THE SPIRIT
WHICH IS FROM GOD

By

Frank Lindblad
6526 LATONA AVENUE,
SEATTLE, WASH.

WIPF & STOCK · Eugene, Oregon

Wipf and Stock Publishers
199 W 8th Ave, Suite 3
Eugene, OR 97401

The Spirit—Which Is From God
By Lindblad, Frank
Softcover ISBN-13: 978-1-60608-184-6
eBook ISBN-13: 978-1-7252-2338-7
Publication date 9/11/2008
Previously published by Gospel Publishing House, 1928

This edition is a scanned facsimile of the original edition published in 1928.

PREFACE

This little work on this important subject does not attempt to completely cover it. Much has been purposely left out, such as the work of the Holy Spirit in glorifying and revealing Christ in the life of the believer. It is rather intended to cover a few facts of interest to those who are hungry for and seeking the baptism of the Spirit, and some of the phenomena which come as a result of the full enduement with power from on High. Much more can be said, and will be dealt with in a later volume on the subject of the person and work of Christ.

FRANK LINDBLAD.

6526 Latona Ave., Seattle, Wash.

CONTENTS

			Page
Chapter	I.	Introductory	11

Chapter II. His Name and Person 15
The Paraclete — The Spirit of Truth — His Deity — A Holy Spirit — A Person.

Chapter III. A Few of His Characteristics .. 19
Above Natural Laws — Everywhere Operative — Infinite Personality — Distance Unknown — Seven Spirits of God.

Chapter IV. His Work on the Sinner 25
Conviction Necessary — Man's Substitute — Works thru Instruments — Things Unnecessary — The Word — The Word Brings Light — Perverted Scripture — Upholds Christ — The Law — Stony Hearts — Continued Conviction.

Chapter V. His Gifts to the Church 40
Provided by Christ — The Body — Apostles Appointed by God — Received Revelation — Given Once — False Apostles — Prophets — C h o s e n by God — Prophetic Anointing — No Turning Back — Evangelist — A Definite Anointing — Hunger for Souls — Self-made Evangelists — The Pastor — A Difficult Office — Unsaved Pastors — Pray for Pastor.

Chapter VI. The Comforter 57
The Comforter Important — Dual Office Work — Glorifies Jesus — His Knowledge Is from God — His Presence Needed — His Work in Us — The Fruits of the Spirit — Led by the Spirit — He Works thru Us — Uses the Gifts — Uses Human Bodies — He Works for Us — In Old Testament — In New Testament — He Works Today.

Chapter VII. Try the Spirits 74
The Test — The Application — Demon Doctrines — A Dangerous Practice — Demonic Healings — Sin Against the Spirit.

Chapter VIII. Is it Scriptural to Seek for More 81
Be Filled with the Spirit — Ask, Seek, Knock — The Samaritans — Paul at Ephesus — Thousands of Others

Chapter IX. Yielding to God 87
Two Forces at Work — Not Against Flesh and Blood — All Believers Have Spirit — The Spirit Leads — Natural Resistance — Our Will Supreme — Our Stubborn Will — Increasing Surrender.

Chapter X. Is the Holy Spirit a Reality? .. 97
An Old Testament Reality — An Early Church Reality — Self-Delusion — It Is Real.

Chapter XI. Why the Power Is Necessary ..104
Demons Worshiped — Tremendous Opposition Met — Power Given — Word Confirmed with Signs Following — Special Anointing — The Promise Fulfilled — God's Power Necessary To-Day — God Not Changed — For Us Also.

Chapter XII. This Is That 118
Shall Be in You — Joel's Prophecy — Unto All That Are Afar Off — Early Church Days — Cornelius' Household — The Evidence.

Chapter XIII. The Infilling and Its Evidence ..127
Not a Plaything — The More the Better — Infilling Is of Value — Yielding Necessary — The Flesh Resists — No Two Alike — Obstacles — Demon Opposition — Complete Surrender — The Spirit Speaks — The Value of Tongues — Not Full Perfection.

Chapter XIV. The General Gifts of the Spirit 138
The Spirit Decides — The Talents Determine — Natures Change — Humbleness Necessary — Fractional Gifts — The Human Will — Why Obtain More — Limiting Factors — For Edification.

Chapter XV. Prophecy 146
Prophecy Greatest Gift — Of Personal Blessing — Like Unto Fire — Refreshing — Virtue Flows Out — Anointing Evidences Call — Easily Quenched — Various Forms — Lesser — Greater — Value of Education — Greatest Form.

Chapter XVI. Speaking with Tongues 163
Compared with Prophecy — Three Forms — Prayer in Spirit — Praise in Spirit — Singing in Spirit — Intensely Edifying — Of Value — Interpreted Message — During Sermon — Clears Atmosphere — Baptism Evidence — Satan Hates — Cause of Opposition.

Chapter XVII. Tht Gift of Interpretation 182
Follows Baptism — Unlocks Mysteries — Imparted Differently — Often Prophetic — Often Misused.

Chapter XVIII. The Gift of Healing 188
An Operation of the Holy Spirit — In Old Testament — In the Atonement — The Age to Come — Available Now — A Definite Promise — Meet Conditions — For Us Now — Works Differently — Salvation Accompanies — Yielding Necessary — Virtue Flows Out — Produces Tiredness — Works at a Distance.

Chapter XIX. Miracles and Powers, Part I 206
Man's Opinion — God Can — All Matter from God — The Spirit Is Able — The Same To-day — Greater Than Healing — Miracles Magnify Jesus.

Chapter XX. Miracles and Powers, Part II 219
Most Powerful Manifestation — Possible Demon Origin — Varying Demonic Power — Insanity — Caused by Sin — Spiritism — Epilepsy — Violence — Faith and Courage Needed — Exceeding Powerful Anointing — Demon against Demon — Method of Procedure.

Chapter XXI. The Gift of Discernment 235
Needed by Early Church — Two Forms — True Form — Our Five Senses — Independent of Senses — Detects Sham — Needed by Pastors — In Praying for Sick — Detects Demon Presence — Senses Spiritual Atmosphere — Is Not Own Thoughts — Not to be Peddled — Needed To-day.

Chapter XXII. Order in the Assembly 249

CHAPTER 1

INTRODUCTORY

This subject, like that of new birth and regeneration, is not easily dealt with. It is a well known fact that the most difficult people to preach salvation to are those who think that they are saved when they are not. Their attitude becomes a cloak or a bulwark which prevents the Holy Spirit from effectually reaching them. The foundations of their false security must first be demolished and cast aside before any real knowledge can be imparted, and often in the course of this demolishing and removal some plain things need to be said.

To a considerable degree the same conditions exist when dealing with the subject of the Holy Spirit. The misinformation, or rather ignorance, concerning the person, the work, and the fruits and gifts of this wonderful individual is appalling. And this ignorance is not limited to people of small education and little experience. It is also found among those who profess the greatest learning and who may have served God for years. Often an uneducated and comparatively newly saved person will have far greater working knowledge of the Holy Spirit than some one otherwise well gifted. The pulpits are often more guilty of this ignorance than the pews.

There is a vast difference between the purely theoretical, and the Biblically practical knowledge on this subject. Our opinion of what ought to happen and what really does happen are often widely divergent. What the Scripture says concerning the Holy Spirit is one thing, but what some man, men, or whole denominations may THINK is often miles away from the truth. Whole denominations, creeds and doctrines have been built up and are being fostered on what some man or men THINK about the Holy Spirit. On the other hand, whole denominations, churches, and thousands of hungry people are being deprived of what God wishes to give to them and what their souls are hungry for, because those who are in power and have rule over them, in their soul-destroying ignorance, profess to be wise. "My people are destroyed for lack of knowledge." Hosea 4:6. How glaringly true in this case, but woe unto them thru whom the perishing comes.

Those who are skilled in teaching tell us that in order to really learn it is often necessary to temporarily lay aside all former knowledge and begin anew. Persons who have studied music by themselves, on employing competent instructors, find that at times the most productive results come thru starting from the beginning. In view of the vast horde of different aspects on the question of the Holy Spirit, with almost no two alike, it might be best to go back direct to the Scriptures, forgetting what man has said, taught, or written, and take an unbiased look at the Word itself.

Most views, doctrines and teachings concerning the Holy Spirit are found to contain only a portion of the great truth. But the peculiar fact is that each individual or aggregation holding its fractional views feels quite certain that it knows all about it and that there is no more to be said. Not seldom the one who has

INTRODUCTORY 13

had his sins forgiven feels absolutely positive that this is all there is to the mysteries of godliness. Another may have gone a little further, but questions the orthodoxy of anyone who claims to have received more than he has. Still another receives a wonderful blessing and experience and whether it is scriptural or not to do so, calls it the baptism of the Holy Spirit, and stops right there. He refuses to go any further, for he is positive that he has it all. He questions even the salvation of any one who does go further and hinders if possible those who try to do so. Each particular little crowd uses the Scriptures to uphold its own stand, and some vehemently fight and oppose those who do not see as they do.

The whole thing looks ridiculous and is in a measure like the blind men who examined and described the elephant. One said that he was like a wall. He had rubbed the side of the big brute. Another said that he was like a piece of rope, a little raveled at one end. He had grabbed the tail. Another said that he was like a tree-trunk. He had gotten hold of a leg. The one who had grabbed one tusk was sure that the elephant was like a bamboo pole, long and smooth. And the last one ran afoul of the trunk and swore that he was like a twisting, supple snake. And then a great strife and wrangling arose. Each one was certain that he was correct, for had he not felt with his own hands and did he not therefore know what he was talking about? The fact of it was that each one was correct as far as he had experienced, but they all made the mistake of not giving credit to what the other knew to be true. But the man who could really see had a complete knowledge of the elephant's appearance, and to him the others' words and actions seemed silly and comical. Are not many to-day like those blind men? Each has a part of the truth, is certain that he is right, and that there is no more to be gotten and that all others are wrong.

Possibly the worst feature of this professing to know it all is that it hinders that person from seeking and obtaining any more. The Holy Spirit gives us only as much as we desire and ask for. If the request is for a little, we receive a little. If we think that this little is all there is to be had, then we never get beyond it. Ask largely and largely ye shall receive.

Taking a fractional view will never get to the real truth in the matter, but accepting the whole truth as contained in the Scriptures will. It is not wise to attempt to lean toward the interpretation of some one creed or doctrine. So many are speaking of their point of view along different lines, mentioning the Baptist, Methodist, Holiness or Pentecostal, or some other. But are not these points of view only man-made? Are they not due to an imperfect and fractional vision of the great whole? A real Holy Spirit illumination of the Scriptures will give but one view—the one brought by the true revelation thru the power of God.

CHAPTER II

HIS NAME AND PERSON

In the 14th and 15th chapters of the Gospel of John there is as much or more information concerning the Holy Spirit as in all the rest of the Scriptures put together. Here Jesus speaks directly concerning Him, and His information is first hand. Paul, Peter and the others also tell of the Holy Spirit, but their information has either come by revelation or by experience, altho neither of these make the knowledge any less valuable. However, Jesus as the Incarnate Word, the Image of the Invisible God, and who received not the Spirit by measure, was more qualified to speak and to give intimate and direct knowledge than any other person.

The Paraclete Jesus, in speaking of the Spirit, calls Him the Paraclete, which word the translators have rendered as "Comforter," and which, without gainsaying, is a good rendering. But it happens that the Greek word "Paraclete" is very rich in its contents, and its full meaning can hardly be passed on thru the medium of just one word. The Greek was a very rich and flowery language, and as a consequence lent itself to the expression of thoughts not capable of full expression in any of the languages of to-day. This word "Paraclete" is one of its meaningful words and means far more than simply "one who comforts." It also implies an advocate, one who walks beside, advice-giver, governor and care-taker. And the Holy Spirit is all of this and even more. He does comfort, is an advocate or pleader, does walk beside, and even indwells, does give advice, and governs and takes care of those who are intrusted to Him; that is, if they will let Him.

The Spirit of Truth   In John 15:26; 14:17 and 16:13, Jesus calls Him the Spirit of Truth. In using the definite article "the" Jesus implies that there are not several true Spirits and the Holy Spirit one of these, but that there is only one, and that the Holy Spirit is that one. It further implies that there is a spirit not of the truth. In John 14:26, Jesus gives Him another name, the Holy Spirit. This tells us that the Comforter is a holy spirit. There are spirits that are not holy, but rather unclean, filthy, sensual, and so forth; but this one, the Comforter, which is from God, is clean and pure.

His Deity   This holiness has a cause. He "proceedeth from the Father." John 15:26. The Father is His source. If there were no Father there would be no Holy Spirit. Now, the Father has as His own attributes, among many others, Holiness, Majesty, Purity, Truth, and so forth. The Spirit, proceeding forth from Him, carries all of these with Him and contains these same attributes. Jesus, the Son of God, the Word made flesh, and in whom dwelt the fullness of the Godhead bodily, possessed the attributes of full Deity, and contains and contained all the attributes of God the Father. As Creator, Jesus received worship which is not allowed to the creature.

Angels, who are created beings, refuse to receive worship, while Jesus, who is Full Deity, accepted it because it belonged to Him. Jesus as the Incarnate God contained life (which is only contained in God) and gives life. The Spirit, who is also Deity, has the properties of Full Deity. He also gives life. "The letter killeth, but the spirit giveth life." 2 Cor. 3:6. "But the spirit is life because of righteousness." Rom. 8:10. "It is the spirit that giveth life." John 6:63. "But if the Spirit of him that raised up Jesus from the dead dwelleth in you, he that raised up Christ Jesus from the dead shall give life also to your mortal bodies thru His Spirit that dwelleth in you." Rom. 8:11.

A Holy Spirit Because God the Father is holy and pure His Spirit also is holy and pure. Because God is the Father of all order and government both among men and in the universe as a whole, therefore the Spirit of God is not the author of confusion. I Cor. 14:33. God is the author of all truth, Ps. 31:5, therefore His Spirit is the Spirit of Truth. The Holy Spirit does not tell lies or inspire men to do so, neither does He give revelations or say things that contradict something that He previously has brought forth. He does not cause confusion or contradictory authority, neither does He cause unholy and obscene words to be spoken or actions to take place. God should always be dealt with in reverence, for "holy and reverend is His name." Ps. 111:9. Likewise the Holy Spirit needs to be respected, for He resents certain things and is easily grieved.

A Person   Altho the Greek word for spirit is a neuter word, that is, it has no gender and is neither male nor female and should call for the impersonal pronoun "it," yet Jesus refers to the Spirit as "Him" and "He." For this there must be a reason. Many have called the Holy Spirit an influence thereby begrudging Him any personality and insisting that He is only the influence of God. God's influence surely is felt thru the presence of the Spirit. But an influence is a dead thing, either exercised by someone else or at his control. A body of men, a country, one man, a corporation, a law, economic conditions, a holy life, climatic conditions, etc., all exercise an influence, but that influence cannot search, talk, reveal, tell of things to come, or give life, all of which the Holy Spirit can do and does. A railroad tie, a fence post, a tree, a mountain, the wind or the moon cannot express any desire or become grieved. Only a person can do this. In the days of the Apostles they said, "It seemed good to the Holy Spirit, and to us." Acts 15:28. Agabus said "Thus saith the Holy Spirit." Acts 21:11.

Jesus said, "He shall guide you into all the truth: for he shall not speak from himself; but what things soever he shall hear, these shall he speak: and he shall declare unto you the things that are to come. He shall glorify me: for he shall take of mine, and shall declare it unto you." John 16:13-14. Here He is called "He" by one who knew Him better than any other human being, one who knew Him since before the foundation of the world and whose expression must stand.

The Holy Spirit is a person.

CHAPTER III

A Few of His Characteristics

Above Natural Laws The Holy Spirit, being a spirit, is not subject to natural laws and limitations that human beings are. We as humans have a material body, and among other things this body is a channel thru which God can test, try and bless us. Still in some respects it is almost a nuisance. It has weight and dimensions and is not divisible, cannot be in more than one place at the same time, and requires time and energy for its transportation. The Spirit, not having any material body, is free from these limitations. He cannot be weighed. He is able to influence a balance if necessary but is not Himself influenced by the force of gravity. Our activities must all take gravity into consideration and as a consequence we are practically limited to the surface of the earth and individually to only a small portion of it. The Spirit is free to go up or down as He pleases, free to move thru the atmosphere, the water, or to the extreme limits of the universe.

He has no dimensions and no place is too small to contain Him, and no place is too large for Him to fill. He can fully dwell in the body of the smallest saint and at the same time fill the whole creation. Whether this property is shared by all spirits was a much discussed question among the learned men of the Middle Ages and is still debatable.

Being a spirit He is not hindered by material obstacles. No walls, doors or barriers can shut out His presence. The only thing that curtails and diminishes His activities and operations is the resistance of human minds and unbelief. Even Satan's forces are helpless before Him when God's saints believe. He can bless a man and His presence can be felt while on a fast-moving train, in an airplane or on a boat in mid-ocean. He will honor prayer offered on a high mountain peak miles above the earth or miles away from any human habitation. In fact, He appears more free to work in isolated places than among the multitudes. A miner several thousand feet in the bowels of the earth or tunneling in the hard granite of the mountain side, finds Him just as real there and also as powerful, sweet and majestic, as in the crowded place of worship or in the sanctity of his own closet of prayer. The sailor in the submerged submarine, incased in the steel shell of his ship and covered with and surrounded by water, finds the Spirit in no way shut out. Water, steel, granite, earth and air in no way hinder or shut out this heavenly visitor. Oh, Hallelujah, what a marvelous provision the love of God has made for us! Paul exclaims, "For I am persuaded, that neither death, nor life, nor angels, nor principalities, nor things present, nor things to come, nor powers, nor height, nor depth, nor any other creature (creation or created thing), shall be able to separate us from the love of God, which is in Christ Jesus our Lord." Rom. 8:38-39. And this love of God "hath been shed abroad in our hearts thru the Holy Spirit which was given unto us." Rom. 5:5. In other words, when led by God thru His Spirit

Everywhere Operative

we can never get into a place or condition too tight or too hard for Him to follow us and be with us. The tighter the place or the condition, the more His presence can be felt and the more He blesses. What a comfort and consolation. The prisoner, the exile, the homesteader on the bleak prairie or in the depths of the dark, dismal winter woods or in the small isolated mountain valley, the patient on the hospital cot longingly waiting for the first glint of dawn, the saved young man or woman in the midst of cursing, swearing, foul-mouthed companions, the soldier or sailor in the midst of battle, the lone missionary miles from a white skin and in the midst of soul-sapping, demon-worshipping heathenism, all are brooded over and comforted by the blessed Paraclete. What a good God!

Infinite Personality Altho the things mentioned are wonderful, there is another still more so. That is His ability and power to be fully present at from one to a million different and widely scattered places at the same time and still not have His power diminished or decreased by this division. Take, for instance, a revival service when the Spirit is convicting of sin. If only one person is under conviction a certain degree of the Spirit's presence is felt. But let two or three or more be under conviction and we find that the presence is in no way diminished. Those under conviction feel no lessening of His operation, but instead an increase. The more there are under conviction and the more material He has to work upon, the more pronouncedly each one feels His workings. Nearly every child of God has noticed this. Or services may be held at any number of places in one city at the same time, and because one place is blessed by His presence it in no way deprives any or all of the others from getting their share. Furthermore, He can and does bless over the whole world, and is present at one thousand or more different cities or countries at the same time, and each one gets not only its share but as much as it has prepared for, whether it be London, Paris, San Francisco, Cape Town, Sidney, Hammerfest or Peking. He is at each and every place at the same time and in the full power of Deity at each place.

On the day of Pentecost He divided Himself upon one hundred and twenty persons at the same time, and each one was described as being filled. Acts 2:4. As a result of that experience Peter could say, "I have the Holy Spirit." Likewise John, Andrew, James, Mary the mother of Jesus, and others. No one of them would dare to say, "Because I have the Holy Spirit it is not possible for you also to have Him." Paul speaks of "the Spirit which he hath given us." So He has become the joint possession of many persons. However, the fact that Peter was filled as he stood up to address the multitudes in no way subtracted from or lessened what John or Andrew or any of the others had. The indwelling Spirit becomes a definite person to the one that possesses Him, and with Him holds conversation and maintains activities every bit as real as tho this person were the only living being that has this experience. He is a real person to each individual, and altho His activities and indwelling presence is spread over millions of persons and in hundreds of places His full personality and Deity is maintained to each person in each instance.

A FEW OF HIS CHARACTERISTICS

Distance With the Spirit of God there seems to be
Unknown no such thing as distance. The Stoneway
Tabernacle of Seattle was broadcasting a
series of services over KOMO, one of the large broadcasting stations. In isolated, scattered and far distant mountains, islands and valleys of the Pacific Northwest, hundreds of Christians met in their homes at the set hour to enjoy the service. If the speaker at the sending station felt blessed then those listening in felt blessed.

One day while sending, the service felt bound and tight. After some ten minutes the speaker undertook to pray. On uttering a few words the Spirit of God came mightily upon him. From hundreds of miles around reports came in that at the same precise moment those listening felt a wave of the presence of God. At another time the speaker felt a definite assurance that he was speaking directly to some one "out in the air." An unsaved man in another city had borrowed a receiving set to try it out. He told a friend, "He was talking right to me and it made me weep."

In Revelation we find these quotations: "From the seven Spirits that are before his throne." Rev. 1:4. "These things saith he that hath the seven Spirits of
God." Rev. 3:1. "There were seven lamps
Seven of fire burning before the throne, which are
Spirits the seven Spirits of God." Rev. 4:5. "And
of God I saw in the midst of the throne and of the
four living creatures, and in the midst of the elders, a Lamb standing, as tho it had been slain, having seven horns, and seven eyes, which are the seven Spirits

of God, sent forth into all the earth." Rev. 5:6. Seven is God's number indicating completeness, and here indicates the completeness and the all-sufficiency of the Spirit of God.

CHAPTER IV

His Work on the Sinner

"And he, when he is come, will convict the world in respect of sin, and of righteousness, and of judgment." John 16:8.

In dealing with the phenomenon of conviction of sin we have a subject that is not greatly understood by even many professed Christians. Convicting of sin is the greatest work the Holy Spirit can *Conviction* do upon an unsaved person, and is prob-*Necessary* ably the greatest of all the Spirit's manifestations. Because of the general ignorance concerning the Holy Spirit's person and work as a whole, and therefore conviction included, the present condition of the general church has been arrived at. The Spirit has been given not only to brood over and care for the church, but also that the church may be added to thru His activities. Because Peter was filled with the Spirit and preached under His anointing the church received three thousand adherents one day and five thousand another day. Acts 2:41 and 4:4. The church's recruits are from the ranks of the unsaved. Before a person becomes a member of the church he must first be saved, and salvation cannot come until that person has first had knowledge and feeling of his sins and has been under conviction. So unless there is a conviction of sin there is no real addition to the church which is the body of Christ. Because of the predominating absence of the Spirit and therefore also of His conviction of sin, the nominal church to-day is to a large extent adding to her numbers unregenerated persons who never have tasted of the grace of God and of the salvation that there is in Christ Jesus.

All conviction is by and thru the Holy Spirit and without Him there is no conviction. There is no other thing or individual mentioned in the Word of God, or that we know of, that can bring an unsaved person to that condition known as conviction of sin. This is wholly the Spirit's work. Men, angels, principalities or powers can do nothing toward this one end except as they are used by the Holy Spirit.

Man's Substitute Because of the lack of the Spirit's presence and the conviction that He brings, men have busied themselves searching for substitutes that will be just as good. But it happens that in this instance there is nothing just as good. The Spirit is not one of several persons or things that bring conviction. He is the only one who can do so. These others are but counterfeits. We live in an age of progress, evolution as men call it. They are attempting to evolute everything in these days. They have wonderfully progressed in the art of killing one another, of committing sin and covering up their crimes, of debauching their bodies and minds and serving the devil in general. Now they are trying to evolute the Scriptures by removing certain portions obnoxious to themselves. They are also trying out this evolution program on the Spirit's work of convicting of sin, but have only succeeded in making a fizzle of the whole affair and incidentally misguiding many people, and possibly sending many to destruction.

Works It is true that the Spirit uses instruments
Thru and can do but little except thru definite
Instruments channels, but these instruments and channels and efforts are of no value except as they are honored by the Spirit's presence and power. The Spirit can and does use men, but no man ever can, or ever will, bring conviction upon any one except as the Spirit may operate thru him. The Spirit can and does use songs, incidents, words of admonition, personally or publicly spoken, the preached Word, and so forth. But these in themselves are helpless to bring any results except as they are tools in the hands of the Spirit of God.

Man, after excluding the Spirit of God in his attempts at soul saving, has dragged in all manner of things. These at times have proved to be excellent instruments for the creation of interest, drawing the crowds and producing great mental and fleshly enthusiasm. But great interest and powerful and widespread enthusiasm do not happen to be conviction of sin. A powerful presence and operation of the power of God will create great interest, draw crowds and produce much enthusiasm, but these in themselves will not bring the presence of the Holy Spirit. God can use some man's strong personality, and most persons that have been used and are being used of God are of strong personality, but a strong personality in itself, except as God honors it, can bring but little results toward real salvation. In fact, at times it may do great damage. Many a preacher's so-called success consists of the use of more than usual natural talents and being born a leader among men, which gifts sway the multitudes. While under the influence of his preaching people feel dominated by his stronger will power and make a profession of religion which never came from their hearts. There has been altogether too much of this done, and thousands to-day have no more salvation than that received thru the shaking of some man's hand or signing some card.

Things Unnecessary Many, in these days, often mistake enthusiasm for an evidence of the presence of God. Because they sing fast, because there are good collections, because many are boosting the cause, because some or many are free in shouting "Hallelujah" or "Amen," because someone jumps and makes much noise, because the preacher works up a tremendous fervor, removes his coat, jumps and runs to and fro, therefore God must be there! God surely is there doing all that He can, or as much as they will allow Him to do, but very often the largest part of all of this is nothing but plain everyday flesh. When the greatest conviction comes there is a hush over the audience and a silence so deep as to be literally felt, broken only by the sobs of those with whom the Spirit is dealing. Even the infants strangely become quiet or fall asleep.

Others will play upon the emotions, telling narratives planned to awaken sympathy and cause tears, and when this condition is on, urge the people to make a decision. Robert Ingersoll could make an audience laugh or weep, but who would dare to say that such weeping was of God? A person may weep because of having his sym-

HIS WORK ON THE SINNER

pathy played upon thru hearing of some poor widow losing her only son or of the death of some orphan child, but that does not necessarily mean that these are tears of repentance. Stirred emotions and tears of sympathy are not always an indication that the individual has a godly sorrow in his heart because he lied, stole, mistreated his parents or served the devil in general, and rejected Jesus Christ. Godly sorrow worketh repentance, and unless there had been godly sorrow for sin there is no true repentance unto salvation. Evidently there are many who know little or nothing of true repentance or salvation.

The Holy Spirit can and does use emotion, and most conversions are accompanied by emotion. When any normal individual becomes fully awakened to the enormity of his guilt before God, the horror of it all usually so overwhelms him that his powers of resistance are broken down and in a flood of honest tears he yields himself to the Lord. Yielding usually causes tears, but tears are not always an evidence of yielding.

The Word How then does the Holy Spirit bring conviction of sin? Altho the Spirit will use anything that He possibly can, His great tool is the Word. The Word is the Spirit's sword and a hammer that breaks the rocks to pieces. Eph. 6:17; Jer. 23:29. He will convict "of sin, because they believe not on me; of righteousness, because I go to the Father, and ye behold me no more; of judgment, because the prince of this world hath been judged." John 16:9-11. Thru the Word, man comes to the knowledge of sin, to his knowledge of Jesus' righteousness, and to the knowledge of the judgment of the prince of this world and of his own coming doom. The Word, or rather our attitude toward the Word, shall be the basis of judgment on the great reckoning day. The Spirit now takes the Word, and using it as a sword, pricks men's hearts, cuts thru the shallow refuge of lies that men are hiding behind, the filthy rags of self-righteousness that men are trying to cover themselves with, and vividly lays bare the secret contents of man's innermost thoughts. Heb. 4:12. Thru the Word, man comes to the knowledge of his sin. Because the Word says, "Thou shalt not bear false witness," "Thou shalt not steal," "Thou shalt not covet," man knows that lying, stealing and coveting are sin. Among some peoples, where the Word is not, there is not this knowledge and to them it is often a credit to do these things. The one who can most craftily lie or steal is the most accomplished man in their midst. Among others the possessor of the most scalps or heads receives the most honor. But when the Word comes and with it a knowledge that lying, stealing and killing are against the wish, will and command of God, this same man, instead of being proud of his achievements, becomes ashamed and downhearted and feels depraved over the enormousness of his guilt. Without the use of the Word it would be impossible to bring conviction of sin upon such people. Missionaries find that it is practically impossible to get any heathen to become interested in any way or feel any need of salvation until they are able to grasp the message of the Word. And in most cases their greatest and hardest work is to develop the minds of the people to this end. Many are unnecessarily criticizing the efforts at educating the heathen, but in many cases it is absolutely necessary to educate in order to put them in a position where they can grasp the truth concerning sin.

The Word Brings Light Instances are on record of how different heathen actually for years sought to come to the knowledge of the true God, but never found Him until some portion of the Scripture came into their possession or they met with someone who knew Him. They tell of how they visited shrine upon shrine, how they punished and tortured their bodies and even their souls in their efforts, but the knowledge of God and the salvation that they sought did not come until they found the Word of God. God surely saw their striving, tears and effort, but the Spirit had no means of imparting the necessary knowledge until the Word became available.

A saved heathen asked how long this knowledge of the true God had been in the possession of the white race. On being told, she exclaimed with great surprise, "And why did you not come over and tell us sooner?" She told how she, herself, had sought Him for years, and that her father had sought Him all his life and died still longing for a knowledge of Him. "The opening of thy words giveth light." Psalm 119:130. The Holy Spirit sees and knows the need of these people, but until the Word is available He is helpless to give these dwellers in the darkness the light they seek.

Not only is it practically impossible for the Spirit to bring men to Christ where there is no knowledge of the Word, but He also has His work curtailed and even at times totally stopped by a perverted knowledge of the Scriptures.

Perverted   Satan knows the value of the Scriptures in
Scripture   bringing men to Christ, so in his efforts
to keep men in that condition in which he
already has them, it is to his advantage and to man's
damnation that the Word should be "illuminated," "explained" and "expounded" in such a way as to rob it
of its true meaning. As a result, we have different
"revelations," "keys to the Scriptures," and so forth,
every one of which perverts the true intent and use of
the Word and robs the sword of the Spirit of its cutting edge. All the new-fangled and hell-hatched doctrines coming to the fore in recent years are but rehashes of former heathen teachings, but adjusting
themselves to the present-day conditions. To get any
following and to cover themselves with a show of godliness, they must incorporate some of the Word, but in
each instance it is not the Word, but rather a prostituted use of its terms and language. What hope is
there of any man's becoming convicted of sin when he
calls it but an "error," and when lying, stealing and
committing adultery are considered but mistakes? They
tell us that when a woman poisons her rival in love
she makes a mistake, or that when a bank bandit murders in cold blood he commits an error. Mistakes,
indeed, but deadly ones, and of the kind that take the
life of the one committing them. A man who touches
a live high-tension wire makes a mistake, but it kills
him. The fact that he did not know the deadly nature
of the current did not save his life. Sin is sin, and
"the soul that sinneth, it shall die." Ezek. 18:4. And
any twisting or turning or lessening of sin's hideousness and horror, and making men believe that it is anything less than it is, is devilish and from the pit. Any

and all religious creeds or doctrines that uphold any
such teachings are from the abyss, let them be called
what they may, or whoever may foster them. What is
the use of telling a person that the blood of Jesus
cleanses from all sin or saves to the uttermost, when
he does not believe that sin is dangerous, or thinks that
Jesus' blood as it flowed on the cross was of no more
value than when it flowed thru His veins, or of any
more value than that of any other human being's or
even an animal's? Without the shedding of blood there
is no remission of sin, Heb. 9:22, and all religions devoid of the blood of Christ are religions, doctrines and
creeds of sin. All their adherents are sinners and shall
die in their sins in spite of their professions of faith
or love, because their lives have not been cleansed by
the blood of Jesus Christ. If the Spirit of God is not
allowed to uphold the blood, He will not work at all.

Upholds Christ   Or what of the man who does not believe in the Deity of Jesus Christ? All men that
are acquainted with His life believe that
Jesus was a good man. But how many believe that He
is the incarnate Word and that He was raised from the
dead? What is the use of preaching a Christ who was
only a good man or who still sleeps in the dust of the
earth? Jesus said, "And I, if I be lifted up from the
earth, will draw all men unto myself." John 12:32.
The Spirit upholds a living Christ, a resurrected Christ,
a Christ who is to judge all the earth, a Christ who
willingly and with foreknowledge of what was to happen from before the foundation of the world gave His
life a ransom for many. And the picture of this Christ,
held up before the man without God, by the Spirit,

brings him to his knees. This Christ pictured by the Spirit draws men unto Himself. Little wonder that men are not getting under conviction or saved and that the Holy Spirit's presence and power are being withdrawn when men are robbing Jesus of all that makes Him Saviour and are holding this stripped and manhandled Christ before the people. The Spirit cannot bring conviction under these conditions.

The The Spirit uses the law, and the law becomes a
Law schoolmaster to show us to Christ. The law says, "Thou shalt not kill," so we know that killing is sin. The law also says that we shall not take the name of the Lord in vain, that we shall honor our parents, that we shall not covet, so we know that taking the name of the Lord in vain, coveting, and dishonoring our parents are sin. The guilt becomes apparent when He continues by showing us that we consequently are to answer for the deeds done in the body, and that as a result of our actions we shall be eternally banished from the presence of God and cast into the Lake of Fire, which is the second death. Then while we are crushed, humiliated and dreading the outcome of it all, and with a godly sorrow reigning in the heart, He continues by showing us that this same Jesus, who shall be judge and before whom we shall stand, has died for our sins and is willing, glad and anxious to forgive. Having done this He has finished His work as far as the unsaved individual is concerned. He can do no more. Now the unsaved one must act, or he will remain unsaved and die a lost man.

Others will deliberately resist the Word. By continuing to do so they get themselves into a very dangerous position. The Word is the Spirit's sword. Any blunting of that sword or ruining its edge hampers or hinders His work. The Spirit, in using the Word, will use different phases at different times. At one time He holds forth the love of God, at another time God's wrath, at still another something else, each time a little different. These different phases are like a quiver full of so many arrows. Now it happens that there eventually is a limit to the avenues to a human heart. When the Spirit has tried them all and finds them deliberately closed in His face, He can do no more for that one. Each phase used and rejected becomes a blunted arrow that cannot be used again for a long time. When a person has deliberately turned down the message of the love of God, that message is useless upon him for at least a season. As a person continues to refuse and reject, arrow after arrow becomes blunted, and the Spirit stands completely helpless to do any more as all available shafts have been turned. Many to-day are as hard as a rock as a consequence, and can go to service upon service in which God's presence is mightily operating and go away untouched. Not that God did not desire to do anything for them, but that they by their continued refusal of every appeal that the Spirit could make, have robbed Him of every instrument that He could use upon them.

Stony Hearts

Even when this condition is arrived at God can work, but in a vastly different manner. When appeals and pleadings fail He often resorts to sterner measures and will use anything that may be able to crush that stubborn resistance and break down that resisting will. The Spirit forces His presence upon no one. No one is saved against his will, but God can at times put a person in a place where he will be willing. A man in a hospital with a leg broken in several places, smiled, was happy and thanked God for the privilege of being run over by a motorcycle. That, he said, made him willing to surrender. A stubborn, rebellious and unsaved son of godly parents steeled himself against every prayer. But when his sterling charactered, soul-winning and praying father breathed out his last on the cot before his eyes, it crushed that stubborn will and he threw himself on his face and made his surrender. How much sorrow, pain and anguish some people would save themselves and others if they only would say "yes" when God calls, and not put it off until the evil days come! Some have so resisted God that He must bring them upon their own deathbeds, and as they realize that their hour-glass of life is almost empty they cry to the God of their fathers or of their own former days, and even then He hears and answers. But in spite of this, there are some who by a continued resisting of the Spirit get into a place where their conscience is seared as with a hot iron. Being past feeling, nothing can touch them, and cursing or smiling they slip into eternity without God or hope in the world. God never intended such an end for any human being, but when they fight away His Spirit that He has sent to draw them, God Himself cannot aid them.

Continued   Still others live under a continued state
Conviction   of conviction of sin and imagine that this state of conviction is salvation. Conviction of sin is not salvation. When salvation comes conviction of sin goes. Conviction rests where there is a

HIS WORK ON THE SINNER

sin. Conviction consists of the feeling of the guilt of sin. Where there is no sin there is no feeling of the guilt of sin. Jesus came to save His people from their sins, and real salvation takes away sin and sins, therefore also the feeling of guilt of it or conviction of sin. Where there is a continued feeling of guilt of sin there is need for an application of the blood of Jesus Christ, which is the only thing than can and does cleanse from all sin. Many, resting under continued conviction, hope to earn favor with God by being good and try to please Him by being good. Nothing pleases God but accepting the salvation that there is in Jesus and as a consequence becoming good because He makes us so.

Conviction is truly a supernatural phenomenon. It is brought about by a supernatural individual and works in a supernatural way. Some, while under conviction, imagine that they are sick. The appetite becomes poor and sleep likewise. A young woman attended a service and went home feeling miserable. She did not care to come back for fear of "getting religion." Much prayer was made on her behalf and after a few days she was saved. On being asked how it had worked, she said that a queer feeling had come over her and this feeling had increased daily. She could eat but little and her sleep was exceedingly restless and broken. During the day the presence of something followed her everywhere she went. At the time of the afternoon prayer service where prayer was made on her behalf while she was at work, she could feel a queer sensation steal thru her whole body, bringing a desire to weep. She was afraid to speak to those who were saved, and a wall seemed to be in front of her continuously which brought the impression, "Thus far shalt thou go and no farther." On getting saved all this came to an end and joy and peace flooded her soul instead.

Another young woman had been to services. While on the way home she began to scream so that her friends thought she was becoming hysterical. All she wanted was to get saved, and before ever getting home she was saved and ran among the neighbors and woke them up at eleven at night to tell them of it.

A young man, on being spoken to in the afternoon, said but little and did not desire to go to the evening services. But in the evening he came. On being spoken to he could not answer and shortly leaned against the wall as tho sick. On being asked to kneel down and pray, he said that he could not as his knees hurt. In a few minutes he literally collapsed on the floor like a stricken man and cried out for salvation. Questioned about his knees, he replied that there was nothing wrong with them except that they became so weak and they trembled so that he could not stand and that they had given way under him.

Another young man attending several services became very desirous of becoming right with God, but seemed held back by something. On the last evening of the campaign as I spoke to him he fell, first to a chair and then headlong upon the floor, loudly requesting mercy. He said that as my hand touched his shoulder a current not unlike electricity went thru his whole frame and broke down all his resistance.

Still another young man attended services several times and as he had a godly sister and parents, much prayer was offered for him and it became visibly evident that the Spirit of God was mightily striving with him. One evening the presence of the Holy Spirit became so strong that the people began to cry out for salvation over the whole audience even before the preaching commenced. The young man hurriedly left. In a few minutes he came back, and bursting thru the door he threw himself into my arms, exclaiming that it was a case of now or never. He told that when he got outside with a companion, he felt as tho there was a powerful force attempting to restrain him from leaving the place, and urging him to go back with the admonition that it would have to be that night or never. He was gloriously saved.

This Spirit of conviction and power of God will often spread over a whole city or a portion of the surrounding country in such a way that God's presence is felt in the very atmosphere. This powerful and widespread presence of God and accompanying conviction only comes as a result of much prayer, and because the place and the people are ripe and hungry for a visitation from heaven. When this comes people get saved in the homes, at school, on the roads, in the fields and in the barns, at work, and some wake up at night calling upon their friends to pray for them. These are visitations from the throne of grace and often only come once in a lifetime.

CHAPTER V

HIS GIFTS TO THE CHURCH

"But unto each one of us was the grace given according to the measure of the gift of Christ. Wherefore He saith, When he ascended on high, he led captivity captive, and gave gifts unto men. And he gave some to be apostles; and some, prophets; and some, evangelists; and some, pastors and teachers; for the perfecting of the saints, unto the work of ministering, unto the building up of the body of Christ: till we all attain unto the unity of the faith, and of the knowledge of the Son of God, unto a full grown man, unto the measure of the stature of the fullness of Christ: that we may be no longer children, tossed to and fro." Eph. 4:7-14.

Provided by Christ Christ, thru His death and resurrection from the dead, made available to us and for us those things which Adam's transgression shut us off from, and more. Thru the Holy Spirit these things are in a measure now being scattered abroad among and upon those who have accepted Christ and have become members of His body. Christ shares with His Body what He Himself has conquered and has become possessor of. So we have become heirs of God and joint heirs with Christ, and this inheritance is made operative in us and upon us thru the Holy Spirit.

By Christ's sacrifice and thru the cross not only did a body of believers come into being, but arrangements were made for caring for that body of believers. Christ has made provision that the general welfare of the body as a whole shall be ministered to by each individual member of it; that thru this ministration the body may grow in strength and stature and may develop into a full-grown man.

The Body Paul uses the human body as a type of the body of Christ. Each part of the human body has its work, some parts little understood, it is true, but there for a purpose nevertheless. There are the limbs to carry it about. Without them it is crippled and needs outside aid to maintain itself. The hands cannot be used for walking to any advantage, and are absolutely incapable of seeing or digesting food. There are the eyes, ears and nose, which sentinels warn of approaching friend or foe, and without which life is hardly worth living. Each has its place and work and when out of order and not functioning properly the whole body suffers. Most headaches and backaches are not in the head or in the back, but simply symptoms of disorders somewhere else. A mashed finger or an abscessed tooth affects the digestion, sleep and the whole body.

In the body of Christ each individual member has a place and a work to do, and any failure to occupy the place assigned or to do the work rightfully belonging to it, causes pain or disorder in the whole body. Have you ever had to breathe thru the mouth while having a severe cold? Yes, it worked after a fashion, but there came a great feeling of relief when the nose again did what it was supposed to do.

Thru the Spirit's dividing unto each one severally as

He will, each member of the body of Christ has received an assigned place and the necessary power to properly do its work. To some He gave to be apostles; some, prophets; some, evangelists; some, pastors and teachers; that each one of these so appointed might fill the place assigned, and to each one was given the necessary power and gifts to properly fill this place. And all of these were given that the Body as a whole might profit by it and grow, be edified, come to a full knowledge of Christ, and no longer be children, tossed to and fro by every wind and devilish doctrine that blows. Each one has a ministry and thru this ministry the body is cared for and developed. In other words, it is thru these human instruments that the Holy Spirit accomplishes His work of caring for the Body, and it is His division of the gifts upon each one of these that determines their office and work.

Apostles Appointed by God The chief among these offices appears to be that of apostleship. The apostle is always mentioned first and appears to have the pre-eminence. Just what true apostleship consisted of as possessed by the original twelve and by Paul is hard to say in this day and age. In the early church, as is also the case to-day, there were those who claimed to be apostles but who were not. Rev. 2:2. But in either case, they have appointed themselves to the office. Real apostleship comes from God and in no instance seems to have been sought for. Paul certainly did not seek it. But still he did not hesitate to claim its full privileges when it became evident to him and to the others that his gifts equaled, or possibly even exceeded, those who were called the chiefs among them.

In the days of Israel the prophets received the message that dealt with Israel, both for their own time and for time to come. Very little was said about the Gentiles or the Gentile age. Since the time of the Gentile adoption which ushered in the present age, which is the Gentile age, the revelation of God's will has been left to the church; and in the church thru the apostles and prophets this revelation has come forth.

Received God's will concerning the Gentiles for
Revelation ages has been hidden. Paul says in Ephesians, "For this cause I Paul, the prisoner of Christ Jesus in behalf of you Gentiles, if so be that ye have heard of the dispensation of that grace of God which was given me to you-ward; how that by revelation was made known unto me the mystery; as I wrote before in a few words, whereby, when ye read, ye can perceive my understanding in the mystery of Christ; which in other generations was not made known unto the sons of men, as it hath now been revealed unto his holy apostles and prophets in the Spirit." Eph. 3:1-5. This knowledge, which before had been hidden, came to Paul by revelation in the Spirit. Just when this came we are hardly in a position to say, but very probably it was given when he was in Arabia "not conferring with flesh and blood," but with Jesus Christ Himself. He wanted his message to be clean of all traditions and man-made doctrines and ideas; and God honored his desire by uncovering hidden things; things fresh, and which were needed for that day and hour. As he was to deal with the Gentiles he needed a message for the

Gentiles. As the old Jewish forms and traditions were not for them, God gave him the message that both he and they needed. God gave not a new patch for an old garment, but a new garment from new cloth.

Given To the apostles God intrusted those revelations
Once of Jesus Christ which since have become the foundation upon which the whole church structure rests. For it says that the household of faith is built upon the foundation of the apostles and the prophets, Christ Himself being the chief corner-stone. Eph. 2:20. By most people it is held that the canon of the Scriptures has been closed as far as we are concerned, and that the revelations given to the early church are all that the church will receive in this age. This very probably is correct. Most of the revelations of the self-appointed prophets of former days and of to-day are at variance with the recorded Word, and therefore cannot be accepted. The Spirit of God never brings a revelation that is contrary to the one that He has already given, for He is the Spirit of truth and is not the author of confusion. These unscriptural revelations are usually the product of some disordered brain or else an inspiration from the pit.

Jesus tells the Ephesian church that she had tried them that called themselves apostles, and were not, and found them false. Rev. 2:2. The Nicolaitan teaching of early days, in which angels and Satan were worshiped, was fostered and spread abroad by a school of false prophets. Almost invariably the self-appointed apostle of both former days and to-
False day has something that is either contrary
Apostles to the Scriptures or else is the truth so distorted as to be as bad as a rank falsehood.

The movements they foster and are at the head of give rise to all manner of error and all too often leave a body of believers living in sin, uncleanness and unbelief which puts them in a condition that is worse than the pit from which they were originally dug, and their last condition is ten times worse than the first. If the motive behind this self-appointed apostleship were uncovered it would usually be found to be nothing more than the selfish desire of some backslidden leader seeking for power, authority and notoriety.

True apostleship is from God and administered by the Holy Spirit. It very probably contained all the gifts of the Spirit in such a measure as to make the apostle a fair and capable judge in all matters pertaining to the church.

Prophets Following the apostle in order comes the prophet. The word "prophet" really implies two things: the forthteller of the truths of God and the foreteller of the future. The prophets of Israel did both, and there is very little difference in the operation of the Spirit in the prophets of old and in those of the early church except in the message given. Prophecy in the new dispensation mostly implies the powerful preaching of the Word while under the influence and partial or full control of the Holy Spirit. Agabus, who bound himself with Paul's girdle, was a foreteller. He told of the things which were to happen to Paul at Jerusalem and of the famine that was to take place. Philip had four daughters who prophesied. Judas and Silas, sent down from Jerusalem to Antioch, exhorted the people, they themselves being prophets. Acts 15:32. They evidently preached the Word, for it confirmed the brethren. Péter, preaching on the day of Pentecost and at the healing of the lame man, being filled with the Spirit, was a forthteller.

Chosen by God A man becomes or is a prophet, not because he desires to be such, or others desire it, or because men have appointed him to that end, but because he is appointed by God and called by the Spirit. He is a prophet because the anointing of the Spirit rests upon him. Amos said, "I was no prophet, neither was I a prophet's son; but I was a herdman, and a dresser of sycomore trees: and Jehovah took me from following the flock, and Jehovah said unto me, Go, prophesy unto my people Israel." Amos 7:14-15. Unto Jeremiah, Jehovah said, "Before I formed thee in the belly I knew thee, and before thou camest forth out of the womb I sanctified thee; I have appointed thee a prophet unto the nations. Then Jehovah put forth His hand, and touched my mouth; and Jehovah said unto me, Behold I have put my words in thy mouth." Jer. 1:4, 5, 9. Elisha's being chosen to take Elijah's place came as a great surprise to him, but he accepted it and even dared to ask for a double portion of Elijah's power and apparently received it.

A true calling of God to be a prophet or a preacher of the Word is always accompanied by an anointing of the Spirit that reveals both to the man and to his friends that God has called him. This anointing at times is so powerful that it actually becomes a driving force and a compelling power. He himself feels it, and others feel it flowing from him.

HIS GIFTS TO THE CHURCH

Prophetic Anointing   With every calling of God there also comes equipment and power to do the work required. No man can successfully preach the Word without this anointing of the Spirit, and very few that are not called will feel any degree of this anointing. Therefore, a person not called of God is practically incapable of proclaiming the gospel of Jesus Christ. But many that are not called are attempting to preach, both to their own detriment and to the detriment of others. This anointing cannot in any measure rest upon an unsaved person, so an unsaved man has absolutely no business to attempt to preach the gospel. Because unsaved, uncalled and unanointed young men are entering the ministry, we have so many of these incapable and uninteresting ministers. This anointing gives power to see into the contents of the Word, also to tell it in such a way that others can grasp it. Without this insight into the contents of the Word and this ability to tell it, any man's attempting to preach will be an absolute failure. Many to-day are preaching who never were called to preach and for their own and others' good never ought to have attempted it.

No Turning Back   The callings of God are without repentance and once a man has been called this calling remains and does not leave. Many, like Jonah of old, are running away from God and are suffering in body and soul. Many have blighted their lives as a result of this running away and it seems as tho the curse of God rests upon everything they attempt to do. The curse will not leave until they yield and say "yes." It is best to say "yes" early, for it will save much anguish. Because many of these called have refused to go; refused to fulfill the place in the body that God has prepared for them, refused to do the work that the body needed done and which the Spirit delegated them to do, the body is itself suffering and souls are going unsaved into eternity. What a tremendous responsibility rests upon a called servant of God!

It appears that God has placed in each one that He has called long before He called them—for He foreknew who would be saved and to whom the calling would be given—certain talents and characteristics which especially fit the person for the work required. Many are using for themselves these talents which God has placed there for the purpose of glorifying His name. They heap to themselves riches, honor, power and a great name, and for this, before God, will have to answer for things that fairly stagger the thought.

And some He gave to be evangelists. This word "evangelist" is used but three times in the whole New Testament. Paul admonishes Timothy to do the work of an evangelist and fulfill his ministry. One of the original Twelve was known as Philip the Evangelist.

Evangelist

Evangelist primarily means one that proclaims the evangel or the gospel. But the fact that it is differentiated from that of prophet, who is also a proclaimer of the gospel, implies that it is a calling separate from the other and therefore containing features which cause this separate classification. True prophecy is not common altho many claim the gift. True evangelism is also uncommon and is vastly different from what many think it to be. Many nowadays are adding this title to their names without knowing what it really implies.

HIS GIFTS TO THE CHURCH

A Definite Anointing   Paul asked Timothy to do the work of an evangelist because in Timothy lay those gifts and upon him rested the anointing which showed Paul that the Holy Spirit had called Timothy to this work. Philip was called the evangelist because his work and the result of his labors proved that the Holy Spirit had definitely anointed him to that end. The evangelist is more than simply a proclaimer of God's general truths. The prophet gives general truths to the saint and sinner alike. The teacher's and pastor's labors are largely limited to those already saved. But the great field for the evangelist is the unconverted. Each gift has an anointing peculiar to itself, and the true evangelist has an anointing peculiar to himself. A bird-dog literally trembles at the sight of a wild fowl and a cat instinctively tries to catch the sparrow. There is something in the animal that drives it to do these certain things. We call it instinct, but let it be called what it will, it is a compelling power. The true evangelistic calling contains an "instinct" for souls and the de-
Hunger for Souls   sire for these that is just as real to the evangelist as the attraction of the bird-dog for the wild fowl or the cat for the sparrow.

This hunger for souls compelled Paul to do what he did. Of course he was willing to be compelled, but nevertheless he felt that something within, which drove him from city to city and from land to land. John Knox felt this when he cried, "O God, give me Scotland, or I will die." It was in Charles Finney when it kept him from his home for months just after he was married. It possessed Moody and others. The possessor of this anointing actually becomes as hungry for souls as his body becomes hungry for food or thirsty for water. And the burden for these souls at times becomes so strong as to drive away sleep and desire for physical nourishment. Others who are not evangelists may also share in this burden for souls, but the evangelist has it as a part of his anointing. There is a compassion for souls in his message that can be felt by saint and sinner alike.

Many are making attempts at evangelism that have neither the calling nor the anointing that fits them for the work. In these days when men have a form of godliness but deny the power thereof, we find this professional type whose efforts are a cut-and-dried formula which is repeated from place to place. Men are railroaded into religion and large numbers know no more of new birth than a Hottentot. A true evangelist and true evangelism are always accompanied by the power of God and real Holy Spirit conviction of sin which produces a godly sorrow working repentance.

Self-made Evangelists   A man does not become an evangelist because some board calls him to that work or because he or someone else puts that title before his name. True evangelism is not possessed by a man because of his beautiful, forceful or flowing language, or because of his having a large corps of workers and plenty of personal enthusiasm, but because God called him as such and gave him the anointing that fitted him for the work. There is a vast difference between personal enthusiasm and the power of the Holy Spirit, but not many are able to discern it.

And God called some to be pastors. The word "pastor" originally meant shepherd. Peter calls himself an elder and Paul speaks of the office of bishop. Evidently these two words as used in the New Testament had the same meaning as pastor. As a shepherd of the flock, the pastor became its servant and ministered to its needs but not necessarily to its desires.

The Pastor No office in the body of Christ entails so much rewardless labor, brings so much abuse from men, and is as filled with misunderstandings, heartaches, burdens, sorrows and almost despairs as that of pastor. When Satan plans mischief for the flock he first attacks the shepherd. If he conquers him the rest is easy. If false doctrine is to be brought in he must first try to poison the leader, and the poisoned leader soon injects the deadly virus into all the unwary and undiscerning.

The pastor stands between God and His people and as ambassador of Jesus Christ has a very high calling. Men fail to recognize the sacredness of this calling and are often too free to pass opinion upon the pastor's work and labor. A true pastor serves God, rather than man or himself, and is more anxious to see God's cause prosper than his own. But such men are scarce.

Because he is an ambassador of Christ, the Lord stands willing to bless him in a way peculiar to his calling. To successfully fulfill his ministry he must not hesitate to give God's message whether the hearers will accept or not. He can profitably possess the spirit of discernment sufficiently keen to detect wolves in sheep's clothing and uncompromisingly deal with such, whether others stand with him or not. In order to well fulfill his ministry he must have a good measure of executive ability and with it diplomacy and tact. It will be to his advantage to walk close to God and wait enough upon Him to know His will in all things, and on knowing it to have backbone enough to do it in spite of all opposition. A spirit of meekness and humbleness well mixed thru it all makes his ministry find favor with God and man. Some men possess all of these requirements and even more, and some much less, but God blesses the labors of them all and rewards them according to the faithfulness of their service.

God deals directly with the pastor in ways often unknown to the flock. Individual members at times woefully lack many things that they ought to have and therefore are in no position to pass judgment upon others, much less the pastor. This brings about a situation in which the pastor is often called upon by God to do things that are not understood by the people and he as a result is severely criticized. They can see what

A Difficult Office

he is doing, but not being in a position to understand his reasons and motives often form incorrect opinions and do and say things that were better unsaid and undone.

Many a pastor, having seen trouble coming and knowing just where it was coming from, tried to warn his people and even took steps to forestall it. Because the people themselves were too obtuse they heeded not his warning and checkmated and even fought his well-meant efforts, and Satan soon made havoc in their midst. This is the history of the downfall of many a local church and assembly.

God jealously guards His servants and they are more than precious in His eyes, therefore the Word says, "Touch not mine anointed, and do my prophets no harm." For their sake He has reproved kings and rulers. This holds just as true now as it did in the early church and in the Old Testament times. Consequently no one can antagonize and fight God's true servants, such as a pastor, without getting into trouble with God Himself. Thru fighting of this sort more than one has blighted his own life and damaged others, and to-day is in darkness and even despair. Many a pastor has gone to an early grave, broken in body and spirit, because of unwarranted attacks upon himself and unneedful burdens for the work which would not have been necessary had the flock, or some members of it, not yielded to the devil in stirring up trouble.

However, let not this be construed as any defense for some of these smooth, slick sons of the devil that have wormed their way into the ministry and who are Satan's own tools and mouthpieces in disseminating all manner of demonical doctrines under the guise and name of Christianity and the Gospel. The sooner these individuals are dealt with in a firm and decided manner, the better. Too many local churches, thru misapplied love and charity have allowed such individuals to remain at their head and have in many cases suffered irreparable damage.

Unsaved Pastors No unsaved person can be a true pastor because no unsaved person can have the anointing of the Spirit, without which it is impossible to preach the gospel. But many unsaved men have entered the ministry and, we may well say, are "attempting" to preach the gospel, for their efforts can never be anything but an attempt. Success before God never will be theirs. If it is a terrific battle for the man with the Holy Spirit's anointing, how shall the one fare that is not even saved? Without the anointing how can he know the contents of the Word which only are revealed by the Spirit? What does he know concerning new birth and regeneration, never having experienced them? To him such expressions as "the power of God" and "victory in Christ" mean nothing. How then can he preach the gospel? He does not preach it, but rather the wisdom of this world and the cunningly devised fables of men. The efforts of this unregenerated ministry are the cause of all the trash and foolishness now heard from the pulpits and of the worldliness of the church in general.

This is the type of ministry that has caused the wholesale influx of unsaved members and has fostered this commercial evangelism because it brought in new members. This has nourished shady, questionable and demonical doctrines and gospelless preaching and teaching because it pleased the influential church members. It has brought these social affairs that have sapped the church of her very life and power and made too many a congregation a social society—a poor one, at that. May God have mercy on some men on the Day of Judgment.

The true pastor has his calling from God, and to God he must answer. He cannot shade or temper his message to suit or tickle the ears of his hearers. For the days are already here when, having itching ears, men heap to themselves teachers after their own lusts. These are the teachers that tickle their ears. He must not allow his own feelings or the feelings of his people to hinder him from doing or saying what the Lord commands him to. But as the days have come when men and professed Christians will not hear the truth, the lot of the true men of God is daily and yearly becoming harder. Pray for pastors that their faith fail not. As a pastor is but a human being and has faults and shortcomings like any other person, any congregation looking for a perfect man to fill its pulpit will look for a long time, for no such man exists. When your pastor does not suit you or the congregation, do not commence an underhanded propaganda for his removal. The next one may be far worse. But rather pray for him, and God by blessing him may make out of him the man that you are looking for. True men of God are yearly becoming scarcer and it is steadily becoming more difficult to be faithful to God. They need all the prayers and encouragement that can be given them. Let us rally to their support.

Pray for Pastor

And some, teachers. This office is the last listed and by many is rated as of little value. However, a general survey of church conditions reveals that God-sent and anointed teachers are both rare and badly needed. A true teacher is as much called and anointed of God as an evangelist or a pastor.

Not everyone can successfully teach. There must first be on hand the necessary equipment. The best foundation is a reasoning and analytical mind. If it has been educated, so much the better. The teacher must first see the thing clearly before he can make it clear to another. If it is not clear to him, why pass the tangled and snarled ideas on to some one else? God anoints the analytical mind and makes it effective. And then there must be the ability to pass the information on. Many can see a thing themselves but that is as far as it goes.

When an anointed teacher is going to put forth God's truths, the Lord's presence anoints his mind to give out and the minds of the hearers to receive. Such a service will usually feel a sweet edifying presence of the Lord. Teachers are very seldom evangelists as these gifts are just about opposites. One pastor will be a good executive and be anointed for evangelism. Another is a good executive and teacher. It is very seldom that a man is both an evangelist and a teacher. If any assembly is blessed with a man that is both, let them be sure to keep him. It is a rare combination and one that is of great edification to the assembly.

CHAPTER VI.

THE COMFORTER

The   Jesus in His farewell talk to His disciples,
Comforter on the eve of His betrayal prepared them
Important for the coming of another One whose ministry was so necessary and important that
He told them, "It is expedient for you that I go away; for if I go not away, the Comforter will not come unto you; but if I go, I will send him unto you." John 16:7. Evidently this other individual, called the Comforter, had a work to accomplish, and His ministry was so necessary that Jesus was willing to leave in order to bring His presence and operations. Jesus goes on to explain what this Comforter will do, and this reveals why His arrival was so important. For His work could not be done by another, and if undone, all of Jesus' miracles and teachings, and the whole purpose of His incarnation would go unheeded and bring no results upon humanity.

Dual   Jesus tells what this work is and divides it
Office into two distinct parts, first, the work upon the
Work unsaved, and second, the work upon the believer. To the unsaved the Spirit shows the need of Christ, and having done so, can do no more unless repentance takes place. To the believer He reveals Christ, God's great and unspeakable gift, whom the believer has received and of whom he has become

a partaker. The work of the Holy Spirit upon the unsaved already having been dealt with in another chapter, we pass on to His operations upon the believer.

Glorifies Jesus Of this work Jesus says, "I have yet many things to say unto you, but ye cannot bear them now. Howbeit when he, the Spirit of truth, is come, he shall guide you into all the truth: for he shall not speak from himself; but what things soever he shall hear, these shall he speak: and he shall declare unto you the things that are to come. He shall glorify me: for he shall take of mine, and shall declare it unto you." John 16:12-14. Let us look at this for a few moments. Jesus calls Him the "Spirit of Truth." This clearly distinguishes Him from the spirit of error. There is only one spirit of truth, and there are many spirits of error. And "he shall guide you into all the truth." What can this truth be that the Comforter shall guide us into? Does not Jesus tell Thomas, "I am the way, and the truth, and the life"? John 14:6. Then the truth into whom the Spirit shall guide us is none other than Christ Himself. Notice the "into." Evidently Christ must be something that we become submerged in, and lost in, and the Spirit is the one who does the submerging. "He shall not speak from himself; but what things soever he shall hear, these shall he speak." This reveals that the Spirit does not come in order to represent Himself, or to talk about Himself, but rather that the purpose of His mission is to represent another, and that His very utterances are given to Him, and as an agent, He passes them on to us. "He shall declare unto you the things that are to come." He becomes the spirit of foretelling.

Let us thank God for the Holy Spirit of promise given to keep the saints warned of coming events and abreast of the movements of the times. At the time of the end "they that are wise shall understand," Dan. 12:10, being made wise by the Spirit of Wisdom Himself. "He shall glorify me." Here we have the great secret unraveled. Christ is the one to be spoken about and declared, "for he shall take of mine, and shall declare it unto you." The Holy Spirit does the declaring and revealing, Christ is the one revealed, and the saints are the ones receiving the revelation. Plain, is it not? Does not Paul proclaim "that by revelation was made known unto me the mystery—of Christ—as it hath now been revealed unto his holy apostles and prophets in the Spirit"? Eph. 3:3-5. He also prays that unto the Ephesians might be given a "spirit of wisdom and revelation in the knowledge of him." Eph. 1:17.

The question arises as to how the Comforter has come to this great knowledge. Paul tells us in 1 Cor. 2:9-12, "Things which eye saw not, and ear heard not, And which entered not into the heart of man, Whatsoever things God prepared for them that love him. But unto us God revealed them thru the Spirit: for the Spirit searcheth all things, yea, the deep things of God. For who among men knoweth the things of a man, save the spirit of the man, which is in him? even so the things of God none knoweth, save the Spirit of God. But we received, not the spirit of the world, but the spirit which is of God; that we might know the things that were freely given to us of God." There we have it. The Spirit searches all things, even the innermost recesses of the

His Knowledge Is from God

Being of God, and has the fullest access to all the thoughts, ideas, purposes, plans and possessions of God the Father and God the Son. The very Word (Logos) and all its contents lie open before Him. And all these things He yearns to reveal to us, and we have the privilege of knowing, if we will yield to Him and His leadings. This Comforter has been given to the church as a whole, and to individuals specifically, in order that to each the mysteries of godliness might be uncovered.

The Word, flesh covered, who is Jesus the Christ, is the Image of the Invisible God, and in Him dwelleth the fullness of the Godhead bodily. In Him also all the treasures of wisdom and knowledge lie hidden, for He was made unto us wisdom from God, and righteousness and sanctification and redemption. All this the Comforter has come to make plain to the believer, for Jesus says, "He shall take of mine, and shall declare it unto you." Little wonder that Jesus said that it was expedient for Him to go away and that He prayed for the Spirit's coming. And wise and blessed are we if we recognize His office work and seek for all of Him that can be obtained.

His Presence Needed Now we see why it was important and necessary for the Holy Spirit to come. Jesus as a man was limited in His scope and field of operations. His conversation was with but a comparative few at a time. But the Comforter, who is a spirit, can dwell in, and speak to, anywhere from one to one billion at the same time. And His abiding presence can keep up a continuous work of revelation. By dealing with each one individually He can suit His conversation, leadings and revelations to the capacity and need of each one, something not possible where one man is dealing with large multitudes, such as Jesus was doing.

Altho all the operations of the Holy Spirit upon the believer bring personal blessing and edification, still His work can be roughly divided into three great divisions: His work in us; His work thru us; His work for us.

His Work In Us Of all these, His work in us is probably the most important as far as the individual is concerned. But not all see this. Many are so anxious to receive gifts and manifestations— which are desirable in their place—that they have totally lost sight of the work that the Holy Spirit wishes to do in their souls. The Spirit has come that we "may be strengthened with power thru his Spirit in the inward man," Eph. 3:16, and this power is not only given to bring strength-for service unto others, but also to bring about certain things in ourselves. True gifts and manifestations of the Spirit bring great blessing when rightly used. But the greatest work of the Spirit upon believers is to develop the fruits of the Spirit, and these it appears are more valuable to the individual than gifts and manifestations.

After Paul has discoursed in the twelfth chapter of First Corinthians on the various gifts and their uses, he winds up by saying, "And, moreover, a most excellent way show I unto you." And in this more excellent way the fruits of the Spirit are the most perfect product of the Spirit's indwelling. He mentions that tongues and prophecy are evidences of but a fractional and incomplete presence of God's power. When the fullness has arrived, as will occur at translation and resurrection from the dead, and "that which is perfect is come, that which is in part shall be done away." 1 Cor. 13:10. In other words, the fullness of God's power will put an end to our incomplete knowledge and bring out in all their glory the great fruits of the Spirit, "faith, hope and love, the greatest of which is love," and which three shall remain and abide. And still he admonishes, "Follow after love; yet desire earnestly spiritual gifts," indicating that a well rounded Christian life consists of a wholesome mixture of both.

The Fruits of the Spirit But the question is asked as to how these fruits are developed. Many try to bring them forth in their own strength and fail. Man-made fruits of the Spirit are flat, tasteless and colorless. They have the pallor of death. They are forced and strained, and at their best are but exterior and do not spring from the heart. Thru salvation and regeneration, which is in itself a powerful work of the Holy Spirit, we have become partakers of God's divine nature. And this divine nature imparted by the Holy Spirit produces the fruits which thru Him come forth as naturally as the grape upon the vine and the apple and orange upon the tree.

"The mind of the flesh is enmity against God; for it is not subject to the law of God, neither indeed can it be. And they that are in the flesh cannot please God." Rom. 8:7-8. So it is plainly seen that the unregenerated man cannot produce the Spirit's fruits any more than a hen can grow hair or a cow grow feathers. But a hen can grow feathers and a cow grow hair without any personal effort except just to go ahead and live naturally. The unregenerated man cannot produce one of the real fruits of the Spirit, for they are foreign to him, but the truly regenerated man can, for they come forth as naturally as his breathing.

In fact, the Spirit's fruit can be called the evidence and indication that regeneration has taken place. Herein lies the great difference between the carnal, or natural, and the regenerated man. The carnal man fights his carnal nature continuously. He tries to be good and to please God, but cannot, for it is too strong for him and he finds that he is its slave and bondservant. But the regenerated man discovers that the indwelling presence of the Spirit combats and overcomes this carnal nature, and subduing it, produces in that man those things which he could not produce himself. Or it may be put this way: the person by yielding has made his own will subject to the will of God, so that the indwelling Spirit lives in him, and thru him, and the life he now lives he lives by the Son of God.

That this Spirit-controlled and fruit-producing life is very necessary is evident from the fact that "he that soweth unto his own flesh shall of the flesh reap corruption; but he that soweth unto the Spirit shall of the Spirit reap eternal life." Gal. 6:8. And "if ye live after the flesh, ye must die; but if by the Spirit ye put to death the deeds of the body, ye shall live." Rom. 8:13.

Led by the Spirit This indwelling presence and operation of the Spirit becomes a real leading. Jesus said, "He shall guide you into all the truth," and this leading becomes the evidence of sonship in God, "for as many as are led by the Spirit of God, these are sons of God." Rom. 8:14. This is wonderful.

What we could not do and it is impossible for flesh to produce, God does and brings forth. "For God so loved the world, that he gave his only begotten Son, that whosoever believeth on him should not perish, but have eternal life." John 3:16. This life in sin, this life in the flesh which causes perishing and which no man in his own strength can stop, God put an end to by sending His own Son Jesus, who conquered sin and forgave us our trespasses. And then thru Jesus He gave us the Holy Spirit that sin might no longer reign in our mortal bodies, but that in its stead the fruits of the Spirit might come forth which produce eternal life. Hallelujah!

"But the fruit of the Spirit is love, joy, peace, long-suffering, kindness, goodness, faithfulness, meekness, self-control." Gal. 5:22-23. How vastly these differ from the works of the flesh. The one is the product of the Spirit of God and the other of man's own wicked heart instigated by the Devil. So God's Spirit has come in order to make His children a separate and peculiar people, different in actions and ways of thinking, in affections, and life from the natural man and those of the world. And this difference He brings about by working in them.

He Works Thru Us   The Holy Spirit is not something that we use, but is rather a person and a rational Being who uses us. To hear some people speak about Him one might believe that He is a tool or an instrument of some kind that the person can turn loose at will or order around at pleasure. This is a great mistake. He moves into us, and then thru the talents inherited and developed, and most of all, the gifts imparted by Himself, He works thru us. So instead of using Him as a tool, we are the ones who become His tools and instruments and He is the power, guide and master of operations.

This working thru us has several limited factors and is directly dependent upon many things. These come under two major headings, the natural ability of the person and the degree of the person's anointing. If any one had to choose between a combination of great personal ability and little anointing, and small ability and great anointing, the latter would most assuredly be the wiser choice. However, a good mixture of both is best. A powerful anointing upon a person of great natural ability produces greater results than the same degree of anointing upon a lesser amount of ability. Thus Paul, with his keen mind and great education, and an anointing to the degree of apostleship, became a more effective and result-producing tool in the Spirit's hand than Peter, who had the same anointing but a lesser mental ability and education. Sometimes a lesser anointing upon a great ability will produce equal or greater results than a great anointing upon a lesser ability. Many will pick out instances of this kind and use them as excuses to show that the greater anointing is not necessary. But they fail to ask themselves what might be the results if this same person, with the great ability and lesser anointing, were to receive a still more powerful anointing or the full baptism of the Holy Spirit.

Uses The Gifts   The Spirit in order to operate thru the saints has placed various gifts in the body of Christ. Some of these are general gifts to the body as as whole, such as apostles, prophets, evangelists, pastors and teachers. These are given for the purpose of ministering to and the building up of, the body. Eph. 4:11-16. These general gifts are produced by special gifts imparted to special individuals. Some of these gifts are present in a minor degree even before the full baptism of the Spirit has occurred, while others are never imparted until afterwards, or come as a result of it. These gifts Paul lists in 1 Cor. 12:8-10 as: the word of wisdom, the word of knowledge, faith, healings, miracles, prophecy, discerning of spirits, divers kinds of tongues and the interpretation of tongues. Thus one combination of these, or all of them together, with a very powerful anointing, produced an apostle, while another combination, or the same one with a lesser anointing, produced a prophet. And so on down the scale, the various combinations and anointings produced evangelists, pastors and teachers.

Thru these imparted gifts the Spirit worked and operated. He put the gift in the person and then living in the person He set the gift in operation whenever He chose, and thru its exercise brought His own presence upon the hearers or those affected. So the human being actually becomes the channel thru which the Spirit flows and the mouthpiece thru whom He speaks, the degree of His effectiveness depending on that person's capacity, and more so, on the degree of his anointing.

Uses Human Bodies The Holy Spirit, being a spirit, has no corporeal body, and in dealing with humans who have a flesh body He must directly or indirectly use such a body, and this He has available in those of the saints in whom He dwells. Thus Peter became His mouthpiece on the day of Pentecost and also when he spoke to the five thousand after healing the lame man. The angel that visited Cornelius would no doubt have enjoyed telling all about the risen Christ, but was not allowed to. A human being was necessary to carry the message, and thru Peter the Spirit spoke. At Ephesus, God wrought special miracles by the hand of Paul, so that sick were healed and demons cast out. Philip, at Samaria, became a veritable trumpet of the Spirit when he proclaimed unto them the Christ, and a little later an instrument in the Spirit's hand to explain to the puzzled Ethiopian the mysteries of the message in Isaiah's prophecy of the coming Messiah.

The Comforter, in order to pray a prayer that is certain to reach the throne of grace, will at times make intercession thru us with groanings that cannot be uttered. Rom. 8:26. Paul says that he will pray with the Spirit and sing with the Spirit. 1 Cor. 14:15. And we know that the Spirit can speak in an unknown tongue; and also in a known language interpret that tongue.

Thus in His operations thru us He speaks, prays, sings, prophesies, interprets, heals the sick, and even casts out demons. We are the instruments, He is the master mind behind it all and the source of the power that accomplishes the results.

He Works for Us Paul speaks about "the exceeding greatness of his power to us-ward who believe, according to that working of the strength of his might, which he wrought in Christ, when he raised him from the dead." Eph. 1:19-20. This is none other than the power of God and the Holy Spirit. This great power not only works in us and thru us, but also for us. As children of God we are in the world but not a part of it, and against us are arrayed mighty and powerful spiritual hosts of wickedness in the heavenly places. Eph. 6:12. These fight against us for the purpose of hindering us from obtaining our inheritance and stunting our growth as Christians, but most of all in order to make fruitless our efforts towards furthering the cause of the kingdom of heaven. Against these our comparatively puny physical and mental abilities and knowledge do not go very far. But the one who is in us, the Spirit of Jehovah, is greater than the one who is in the world, and thru Him we have the victory. He not only blesses the physical and spiritual man to make them effective, but He also arranges the conditions and environment under which we labor. He goes before and prepares those with whom we are to deal and opens the way for our efforts. He nullifies the activities of others who as Satan's direct tools and emissaries are trying to resist our endeavors. Thru His knowledge He knows, and by His great power He sets at naught the best laid plans of the enemy.

In Old Testament   The instances of His working for God's children are almost countless. The spirit of God worked for Gideon when he laid out the fleece for a test, and still more so when He frightened the Midianites so that they slew one another. Judges 6:36-40; 7:22-23. He worked for Jehoshaphat and the Jews when the great multitude came up against Judea and Jerusalem. "For the children of Ammon and Moab stood up against the inhabitants of mount Seir, utterly to slay and destroy them; and when they had made an end of the inhabitants of Seir, every one helped to destroy another." 2 Chron. 20:23. He worked for Hezekiah and the inhabitants of Jerusalem when Sennacherib, the king of Assyria, came to kill and make slaves of them. "And Jehovah sent an angel who cut off all the mighty men of valor, and the leaders and captains, in the camp of the king of Assyria;" so that in the morning one hundred and eighty-six thousand were found as dead bodies. 2 Chron. 32:21.

The life of Daniel and his friends and many others were threatened because Nebuchadnezzar's dream could not be revealed or interpreted. After praying "was the secret revealed unto Daniel in a vision of the night." Then Daniel blessed the God of heaven, saying, "I thank thee, and praise thee, O thou God of my fathers, who hast given me wisdom and might, and hast now made known unto me what we desired of thee." Dan. 2:19, 23. The Spirit of God worked for them. He closed the mouths of the lions during Daniel's imprisonment with them for the night. But this curbing of the lions' carnivorous nature was removed when the enemies were thrown in, for "the lions had the mastery of them, and brake all their bones in pieces, before they came to the bottom of the den." Dan. 6:22-24. The Spirit of God in a most convincing manner showed His power to help those who trust in Him when He quenched the fury of the flames upon the three Hebrews in the furnace. The terrible heat necessary to melt metal consumes and destroys such things as clothing and flesh in a few moments. But in this case the natural processes of nature were checked and some unseen and supernatural force and power let them go thru untouched, so that their hair was not even singed, nor was there the smell of fire or scorching upon their clothing. However, this protection did not cover the ropes which bound them, for they were consumed. Little wonder that the despotic and strong-minded king Nebuchadnezzar and his great men were astonished. Dan. 3.

In New Testament Nor was this working of God's power limited to Old Testament times. Wicked Herod had killed one apostle and was determined to kill another. "And when he had taken him, he put him in prison, and delivered him to four quaternions of soldiers to guard him; intending after the Passover to bring him forth to the people. Peter therefore was kept in the prison: but prayer was made earnestly of the church unto God for him. And when Herod was about to bring him forth, the same night Peter was sleeping between two soldiers, bound with two chains: and guards before the door kept the prison. And behold, an angel of the Lord stood by him, and a light shined in the cell: and he smote Peter on the side, and awoke him, saying, Rise up quickly. And his chains fell off from his hands. And the angel said unto him, Gird thyself, and bind on thy sandals. And he did so. And he saith unto him, Cast thy garment about thee, and follow me. And he went out, and followed; and he knew not that it was true which was done by the angels, but thought he saw a vision. And when they were past the first and the second guard, they came unto the iron gate that leadeth into the city; which opened to them of its own accord: and they went out, and passed on thru one street; and straightway the angel departed from him. And when

Peter was come to himself, he said, Now I know of a truth, that the Lord hath sent forth His angel and delivered me out of the hand of Herod." Acts 12:4-11. The angel was God's messenger, but God's power had done the work. The incessant prayer of the church had set in motion the mighty power of the Spirit against which soldiers, chains, doors, gates and guards were of no avail. The unseen, supernatural power of God had broken the chains, and without a flare or candle, had made a light to shine in the cell without awakening the soldiers. The two soldier guards had either slept, for which the penalty was death, and which penalty they later paid, or had been made temporarily blind. Or else Peter and the angel were for the moment invisible. And unseen, supernatural hands had unlocked and swung open the great iron gate. In other words, the power of God had worked for Peter.

He worked for Paul after the serpent had bitten him, so that he neither swelled up nor dropped dead as they expected. Instead it opened the way for reaching the people with the gospel. He works for us to-day in a thousand ways, some of which we know and some of which we do not. He worked for a missionary in South America, who was tired and sick himself, and with his family in need, by speaking to a farmer in South Dakota. This farmer, a stranger and poor himself, accidentally picked up a paper and saw this missionary's name. Instantly the Spirit admonished him to send some funds to the man in South America, which he did. Four weeks later it arrived, just when it was badly needed. In advance God had made arrangements for his need. A Christian in India had been given some food by a Mohammedan. A few days later this

Mohammedan returned and was surprised to find the Christian well and sound. After asking some questions he left. Some time later he confessed that he had put enough poison in that dish to kill ten men. In another instance, a man was to take an early train and set his alarm clock accordingly. During the night he dreamed that the train had been wrecked, and this so impressed him that when the alarm went off he decided not to go that day, but to wait until the next. The next day he went, and then found that the train that he should have taken had been derailed, with great loss of life, and the scene was just what he had seen in his dream.

He Works To-day   When unknown and unseen danger is approaching He puts it upon others to pray for us. A man in a wood-working establishment was fastening some knives on a planer. In some way the idling belt began to slip onto the power pulley while his hand was caught. He said that he never knew how his hand got out without being cut off. Some half an hour before that time a saintly mother in Israel felt strongly impressed to pray for this man, feeling that he was in great danger, and this she did until the burden lifted.

A very ungodly man's wife was saved. This so angered him that he threatened to kill her and attempted to do so. He also carried a loaded revolver for some weeks, and later confessed that he had planned to kill the preacher also. One night, just as he was retiring, and while the light was still on and he was wide awake, he had a vision, in which he saw Jesus coming and taking the saints away and found himself left. This so worked on him that in a few days he was saved. In the same place a gang of some thirty rowdies started for the meeting place to beat up the minister. On the way they stopped at a saloon for a few drinks, so as to have plenty of courage. Altho but little liquor was consumed, in less than ten minutes over half were too intoxicated to stand, and the others had their hands full taking care of them. They never arrived at the meeting place and the preacher knew nothing about it until a week later. Neither these rowdies nor anyone else ever managed to discover how so little liquor could render them so helpless in so short a time.

We little know how many times God undertakes in our behalf and how much evil that was headed our way is sidetracked. Yes, He works in us, thru us, and for us. To Him be the glory forever. Amen.

CHAPTER VII

Try the Spirits

In these days when history is made overnight as it were, and the whole world is in perplexity religiously, as well as politically, great care needs to be exercised in approaching any apparently new religious thought or idea, lest it be found to be demonical in its origin, and one become hopelessly ensnared unawares. However, this timidity and caution can go too far, and there are those who not only fear the false but also refuse the very genuine. And this some have done. With too many, everything supernatural is of Satan, while with others, everything supernatural is of God. However, we know that these two extremes cannot both be true. And to discover which part of the supernatural is of God and which is of Satan we must go to the Word of God.

The Test In the early church they had conditions paralleling those of to-day. This is what the apostle John has in mind when he says, "Beloved, believe not every spirit, but prove the spirits, whether they are of God; because many false prophets are gone out into the world. Hereby know ye the Spirit of God: Every spirit that confesseth that Jesus Christ is come in the flesh is of God: and every spirit that confesseth not Jesus is not of God: and this is the spirit of the antichrist, whereof ye have heard that it cometh; and now it is in the world already." 1 John 4:1-3. This passage makes three great truths evident; first, that there are spirits in the world, among and in men, other than the Spirit of God; second, that these spirits are divided into two opposing classes, with the Holy Spirit on the one side and all the other spirits on the other; third, it gives the test to be applied and states that the spirit which magnifies Christ is of God and is therefore the Holy Spirit, and the ones which nullify Him are not of God, and must therefore be demonical in their origin and relations.

The Application John definitely states that many false prophets have gone out, and we might add that many are still going out and are now working, and will continue to do so until the Lord comes. A prophet in the true sense of the word is endued with the gift of prophecy as the result of being ruled over or dominated by some spirit. Thus he is a prophet of God if dominated by the Spirit of God, and the prophet of Baal, or his like, if actuated by a demon. And the prophet's message reveals the nature of the spirit under whose control he is and by which he is inspired. If, while under the control of a spirit, the prophet praises, magnifies and glorifies Christ and acknowledges that He is the very God in the flesh, then the spirit operating thru him is the Spirit which is from God. If on the other hand, while under the control of a spirit, the prophet gives a message written or spoken that annuls Christ, denies His Deity and all that goes with it, then his spirit is that of the Antichrist or against Christ and is demonical and from hell.

Let us see how this test works upon some of the religions and movements of our day and other days. Most of these have had some prophet or inspired leader and these have had some distinctive message. Here we might mention Buddhism, Mohammedanism, Theosophy, Swedenborgianism, Mormonism, Christian Science, Russelism, and even others. The doctrines of all these have in common the one great theme of the overthrow of true salvation and regeneration and substituting something of their own instead. And to do this they attempt to annul the Deity and atonement of Christ. Therefore, the spirit that inspired these teachers and brought forth these teachings is not of God, but is that of the Antichrist, and the father and instigator of them all is the devil himself.

Demon Doctrines

Swedenborg claimed that he was visited by a spirit and sent into trances and had visions. Mohammed claimed that a spirit named Gabriel came upon him. John Smith, the father of Mormonism, likewise laid claim to having a spirit visitor. The Buddhist priests and devotees of to-day go under the control of various spirits, and while under this control rave and sing and utter prophecies. Various spiritualistic mediums and leaders in Theosophy become periodically possessed of supernatural powers and while under their control have spoken and written all manner of annulling and degrading things against Christ: In view of the lives and teachings of these prophets, and the results of these teachings upon their believers, can their spirit be of God? No doubt they have been inspired, but by whom?

Many unsaved and even some professed children of God, not knowing the dangerous character of these

TRY THE SPIRITS

teachings, often too freely absorb them and before they are aware of it are brought under the influence of their demonical nature. Once under these influences it is very difficult to get out, as Satan is very reluctant to release anyone that he has in his power. A common characteristic among them is their blinding and benumbing nature. A person under their influence is practically shut off from the real truths of the Word because of being brought into a state where he is unable to grasp them. When these teachings speak about God they do not mean Jehovah of Hosts, but rather some first cause, or divine principle, or something else. When they speak of Jesus they do not mean the Christ, but rather a good man. And the atonement they have no use for and do not want to hear about.

A Dangerous Practice On the other hand, some people altogether too quickly pass judgment upon things with which they are unacquainted and before they have applied any scriptural tests. According to the Word, among the manifestations of the Spirit there are prophecy, discernment of spirits, the working of miracles, gifts of healing, and divers tongues with their interpretation. As these workings of the Spirit are not common many Christians are ignorant of both their existence and manner of operaation. On seeing them in use they recognize the working of some supernatural power, but not knowing that God can produce these things they attribute the phenomena to the devil.

Herein lies a great danger. Jesus after casting out a demon was accused by the Pharisees of doing so by the power of Beelzebub the prince of the demons. Matt.

12:24. He let them know that in so doing they indirectly gave Satan credit for the working of the Holy Spirit and that this is blasphemy against the Spirit of God, which sin will not be forgiven in this age, nor in the one to come. If the Pharisees stood in danger of that sin in their day, how much more do people stand in danger of that sin to-day? After almost two thousand years of the Holy Spirit's operations and the clear Word of God, men are now without excuse. Many have been too free with both their written and spoken utterances, and are in great danger of putting themselves in the same position as the Pharisees.

Let us hold on to the Word of God. In so doing we must acknowledge that any person who under the control of some supernatural power is glorifying Christ and attesting to His Deity is actuated by the power of the Holy Spirit. Satan never yet has glorified Christ and does not inhabit humans with his demons for the purpose of doing so. Flesh will enter in at times and becloud the issue. But there is a vast difference between the actions of the flesh and those of either the Holy Spirit or the devil, altho the flesh lends itself at times to the latter to the detriment of God's work.

The test can also be applied to the phenomenon of healing. Thru the prayer of faith, or the laying on of hands in the name of Jesus, God can and does heal the sick, either as a gradual improvement or an instantaneous operation of the Holy Spirit. Satan can also, thru his power, accomplish deliverances which at times are wonderful. Not that he has power to *Demonic* heal directly. It seems that in some cases *Healings* where disease or a disorder is caused by demonical activity a greater and more powerful demon can set at naught the influence of a smaller one, and thus incidentally deliver the one afflicted. This method was used by the ancient Egyptians and is still used by the witch doctors of various heathen races.

Jesus says of an unknown wonder-worker, "Forbid him not: for there is no man who shall do a mighty work in My name, and be able quickly to speak evil of Me." Mark 9:39. In other words, no one can call upon the name of Jesus and have that degree of faith that will open the way for the Holy Spirit to operate thru him for the healing of the one that is sick; and then shortly be so yielded to Satan as to be able to speak evil of Jesus. If in faith the name of Jesus is called over the one that is sick, for his deliverance, then Christ, that His name may be glorified, sets in motion that measure of the power of the Spirit that will heal, or deliver, the one afflicted. Satan never lets go of one in his power unless compelled to do so by one stronger than himself. And he never has, and never will of his own accord, or thru the activities of his demons, release any of his victims at the mention of the name of Jesus unless forced to do so by the power of God.

When healing takes place thru the invoking of the name of Jesus, it is the power of the Holy Spirit that performs it. And the manifestation takes place in order that Jesus Christ may receive the honor and the glory. Here again lies a great danger in that many attribute to Satan the working of the Holy Spirit, quite often for no other reason than that they are personally opposed to the human instrument thru whom God is working; or because they are fighting or attempting to discredit his ministry.

Sin Against The Spirit Any person who, directly or indirectly, willfully opposes the operations of the Holy Spirit puts himself in a dangerous place and condition. First, there is the danger of committing the unpardonable sin for which there is no forgiveness. Satan, of course, is very busy trying to get many to believe that they already have done so when they are absolutely guiltless of any such thing. But, nevertheless, there are those who have committed it, and it is from this class that the modern Christless religions are fed and find so many recruits. The Holy Spirit also is easily grieved, and once driven away is not quickly wooed back again. This produces a hardness of heart that is more or less untouched by anything. It also produces a state of spiritual blindness that completely darkens the intellect. We read how that the god of this world has blinded the eyes of the unbelieving. And many by resisting and opposing the Spirit of God have put themselves where the god of this world, who is Satan, has so blinded them that they have eyes and see not, ears and hear not, and their heart is waxed gross, and their understanding completely darkened to the deeper things of salvation and all the workings of the Holy Spirit. Many who were once powerfully active for God and richly blessed in His service are now in this condition. It is better to be safe than to be sorry, so the advisable thing is to remain silent on the things of this nature if not understood.

CHAPTER VIII

Is It Scriptural to Seek for More?

If the Holy Spirit has been given to the church, is it right for anyone to seek for "more of the Spirit"? Should we not be satisfied with what we have and not tempt God by asking for more? Some seem to be under the impression that asking for more of the blessed Comforter is presumptuous.

Be Filled With the Spirit Paul admonishes that we "be filled with the Spirit." Eph. 5:18. Did not Paul know that all saints have the Spirit? Then why did he admonish them to be filled with Him? Evidently he must have had in mind some other than the initial imparting received at salvation. This strong suggestion which is almost a command implies, first, that there is a condition in which a person can have the Spirit and not be filled with Him; second, that this infilling is what the saints need; third, that there is a method or means by which the one so desiring can arrive at this condition of being filled; fourth, that it is scriptural and in the will of God to seek to be filled; and fifth, that the seeking will not be in vain.

Jesus, in the eleventh chapter of Luke, after teaching His disciples how to pray, tells them about the man who came by night to borrow bread. And then He gives them this direct-to-the-point promise: "Ask, and it shall be given you; seek, and ye shall find; knock, and it shall be opened unto you. For every one that asketh receiveth; and he that seeketh findeth; and to him that knocketh it shall be opened." Of course, these promises hold true for any asking that is according to the will of God. But Jesus also makes these promises very specific when He says, "If ye then, being evil, know how to give good gifts unto your children, how much more shall your heavenly Father give the Holy Spirit to them that ask Him?" Evidently then, the Holy Spirit is given thru the asking for it. This surely does not mean an asking for the imparting of the Spirit given at salvation for the sinner knows nothing of the Spirit before conversion, and how can he have a hunger and desire and ask for something which he knows nothing about? It is rather the asking for a greater fullness of the Spirit that a person yearns for after once having tasted of Him. The whole purpose of Jesus' discourse is to show that the Father will answer the requests made, and that it is absolutely correct to be importunate in asking. And also that God is very anxious to give His Holy Spirit, and that this giving can be brought about by importunity and insistent asking. How then can it be wrong to ask for the Holy Spirit when God both desires and promises to give Him?

Ask, Seek, Knock

Even if there were not these promises there would be encouragement in looking to the experience of thousands of saints of this and past ages whose seeking has been rewarded by receiving more of the Spirit's presence in their lives. Their seeking must have been according to the will of God or He would not have given them what they asked for. John says that "if we ask

IS IT SCRIPTURAL TO SEEK FOR MORE?

anything according to His will, He heareth us." 1 John 5:14. He must have heard or they would not have received, and He would not have heard if it had not been pleasing to Him.

Another may ask if it is scriptural to receive an additional infilling of the Spirit apart from what was given at salvation. What saith the Scriptures?

The persecution that arose after the stoning of Stephen scattered the saints abroad and Philip found his way into Samaria, a region hitherto untouched by the gospel. "And the multitudes gave heed with one accord unto the things that were spoken by Philip, when they heard, and saw the signs which he did. For from many of those that had unclean spirits, they came out, crying with a loud voice: and many that were palsied, and that were lame, were healed. And there was much joy in that city." Acts 8:6-8.

The Samaritans Did the Samaritans become saved? Let us see. Does it not say that they with one accord gave heed to what he said? What he preached was Christ and Him crucified and raised from the dead, and this they believed. If they gave heed they must have confessed their sins and repented. This is what gave them their new-found joy, together with that of seeing their friends and relatives liberated from the power of the devil, for the unsaved do not rejoice over God's working among sinners. Yes, salvation came to Samaria.

"Now when the apostles that were at Jerusalem heard that Samaria had received the word of God, they sent unto them Peter and John: who, when they were come down, prayed for them, that they might receive the Holy Spirit: for as yet it was fallen upon none of them: only they had been baptized into the name of the Lord Jesus. Then laid they their hands on them, and they received the Holy Spirit." Acts 8:14-17.

Paul says in Romans 10:9 that "If thou shalt confess with thy mouth Jesus as Lord, and shalt believe in thy heart that God raised Him from the dead, thou shalt be saved." These Samaritans had believed that Jesus was risen from the dead, for that was Philip's message, and to this they had given heed. And by offering themselves as candidates for baptism they had gone on record before heaven, men and all hell as acknowledging Jesus as Lord. In other words, they had fulfilled all scriptural requirements for salvation and their joy evidenced that they had it. And they had fulfilled all present-day requirements for that matter, too, for many call themselves saved and are considered saved on less qualifications than these. Now when Peter and John came down there they knew all this, and also knew that these Samaritans as newly saved people had already been made partakers in the Holy Spirit, and still they prayed that the Holy Spirit might be given them. So this experience of having the Spirit fall upon them must have been something different and greater than what they already had passed thru or possessed. And God heard the apostles' prayer, for they laid their hands upon them and they received the Holy Spirit. This prayer must have been according to the will of God and the experience scriptural or God would never have heard or honored it.

"And it came to pass, that, while Apollos was at Corinth, Paul having passed thru the upper country came to Ephesus, and found certain disciples: and he

IS IT SCRIPTURAL TO SEEK FOR MORE?

said unto them, Did ye receive the Holy Spirit when ye believed? And they said unto him, Nay, we did not so much as hear whether the Holy Spirit was given. And he said, Into what then were ye baptized? And they said, Into John's baptism. And Paul said, John baptized with the baptism of repentance, saying unto the people that they should believe on him that should come after him, that is, on Jesus. And when they heard this, they were baptized into the name of the Lord Jesus. And when Paul had laid his hands upon them, the Holy Spirit came on them; and they spake with tongues, and prophesied. And they were in all about twelve men." Acts 19:1-7.

Paul at Ephesus   This event occurred years after the initial outpouring of the Spirit on the day of Pentecost, which event many say has made all believers partakers in the Spirit and that there is no further experience to be looked for. These men thru hearing Paul's testimony believed on Jesus, and being baptized fulfilled all requirements and became fully saved even if they were not considered as such before. According to the teaching that all are made full partakers of the Spirit at salvation, then these men became filled with the Spirit the instant they were baptized. Why then did Paul, who surely knew his business, go thru the performance of laying his hands on them when they already had the Spirit? And why did the Lord see fit to honor this by giving them an experience identical with what the apostles themselves had received on the day of Pentecost? Did Paul make a mistake and then did the Lord add to the confusion by making another one? Oh, foolish men, and slow of heart to believe in all that the prophets have spoken!

Thousands of Others And what about the testimony of the lives and experiences of men and women of God who tell of living for years with a knowledge of forgiven sins but at the same time with a longing for something more in their lives, which longing has been satisfied by a mighty outpouring of the Holy Spirit upon them? Or what of the ministers of the gospel who have given forth the Word, but feeling a lack of power have been supplied this by a deluge of God's Spirit upon them even after years of service? Take Moody, for instance, who told how after many years of preaching, he felt a need and a hunger for more of God and how that after a season of waiting on God the power of the Spirit came upon him so mightily that he had to ask God to stay His hand. Two years after this experience he testified that he had accomplished more in those two years than in all the years previous. Charles G. Finney, a short time after his conversion, was so mightily filled with the Spirit as to be beside himself for a season.

It is to be noticed that they who have been clothed with power from on high never deny the scripturalness of such an experience, but it is rather those who have not. Is it possible that those who have not are trying to belittle what God has done for the others, or is it that they are trying to justify the leanness of their own souls? How anxious some are to defend their own condition and what manner of arguments and excuses are dug up to do so. But what they do succeed in doing is to grieve the Holy Spirit and thereby effectually shut themselves off from this blessing. They also dwarf their own souls and bring a hardness upon themselves which is very dangerous.

CHAPTER IX

YIELDING TO GOD

Thru the salvation provided by His Son, Jesus Christ, God hath "delivered us out of the power of darkness, and translated us into the kingdom of the Son of His love." Col. 1:13. We have been moved out from under the dominion of one and placed under the guidance of another. Satan's control over us has been broken and we have yielded to the influence of God's

Two Forces At Work Holy Spirit. This power of darkness under which control we slaved, more or less dominates the lives of all who are unregenerated. The degree of the enslavement is determined by the degree in which sin reigns in that life.

Paul says that we once "walked according to the course of this world, according to the prince of the powers of the air, of the spirit that now worketh in the sons of disobedience." Eph. 2:2. If genuine salvation has taken place in a life, that person no longer walks according to the course of this world but has come out from it and has become separate. He no longer is dominated and influenced for evil by the Satanic inhabitants of the atmosphere which now so busily reign and rule in the hearts and minds of those disobedient to God. But instead he has subjected himself to the Spirit which is good, and which operates in him for his and others' welfare; for "as many as

are led by the Spirit of God, these are sons of God."
Rom. 8:14. So two mighty forces, unseen but not
always unfelt, are keenly active in influencing men for
good or bad, one working to the end of dragging men
to the Lake of Fire and the other bringing men out of
sin and its bondage, and into the glorious light and
freedom of the gospel.

Thru salvation we have changed masters. By the
power of God we have been set free from the dominion of Satan. We tried by exercise of will power and
other means to break this dominion over us, but each
and all attempts were failures; for the one who held
us bound was more mighty than we were. But God,
who is almighty, exercised His unlimited power.
Against this, Satan, altho strong, could not stand, and
we who were in his clutches were liberated.

Not Against Flesh and Blood — If Satan left us alone after his power over us became broken, all would be well, but such is not the case. Altho Satan's dominion has ended he still hopes to recapture his once faithful slave, and to this end does all in his power to get his former victim back under his domination. So the Christian experience becomes a battle "not against flesh and blood, but against the principalities, against the powers, against the world-rulers of this darkness, against the spiritual hosts of wickedness in the heavenly places." Eph. 6:12. A mere man, battling against this list of supermighty antagonists, could expect nothing other than complete and utter defeat, and this certainly would quickly take place unless he received aid greater than what man can give. The only thing that can successfully battle and overcome these unseen powers is another unseen power more mighty than they, the Spirit of God. Altho Satan's power is very great and almost without limit, yet God's Spirit is his master, for God is almighty and His power infinite. This Holy Spirit God has given to all who are members of the body of Christ, which is the church, and all believers possess this Spirit in a greater or less degree.

There are many reasons why God has imparted His Spirit to His children, and possibly one of the greatest is that they might receive power to resist and fight against the powers of darkness. For Jesus says, "Ye shall receive power, when the Holy Spirit is come upon you." Acts 1:8. We all consider the receiving of this power a great privilege, but it is really more than a privilege, it is a necessity. For without it, it is impossible to conquer sin or temptation and futile to attempt any work for the Lord. It is true that a few minor sins and temptations may be overcome by will power, but real victory over sin as a whole can only be gotten thru the power of the Spirit of God.

Some persons may attempt service for the Lord by use of their own natural talents with mediocre success. Such will always feel a lack of something in their lives, but which lack they cannot always explain. And quite often they will notice that others possess that something which they themselves feel the lack of, and it is the possession of this something which makes the other's efforts a success while their own are failures. Successful work for the Lord cannot be accomplished except by the Holy Spirit's operating thru the man, or the vessel, used. Satan is very busy, anxious and determined to corrupt every Christian life and to nullify and checkmate every Christian effort at service. Unless these efforts on his part were counteracted by some power at least equal to his own, his attempts would be very successful. But having God's Spirit to deal with, his efforts are stalled, and often so turned around as to become a blessing. For God can make all things work together for good to them that love Him.

In view of this, about the only conclusion that a person can come to is that the presence of the Holy Spirit is needed in every life and that without Him the Christian life would soon cease to exist.

All Believers Have Spirit But someone says, "Has not the Holy Spirit been imparted to all believers? then what need we more?" The Holy Spirit has been imparted to all believers for without Him no salvation could take place or exist. The very witness of salvation comes thru the Holy Spirit. The Spirit Himself beareth witness with our spirit, that we are children of God. Rom. 8:16. The Spirit has been given to the church, the Ecclesia, the called-out ones, and all who have been cleansed by the blood of Jesus are members of the Lord's body and therefore partakers of the Holy Spirit. But while all are partakers some apparently have more than others, and some have even gotten to the place where they are literally "filled with the Spirit." How can this be and what determines this? Let us see.

Satan is an evil spirit. God's Spirit is a holy spirit. Altho their operations are exactly opposite in purpose and results, yet the conditions and methods of their working are very closely alike. Satan thru sin plunged the whole race under his bondage and he has used this same thing, sin, to increase his hold upon the individual sinner. It is only thru sin that Satan gets any hold on a man. On a sinless life he has no hold. Because Jesus was sinless the prince of this world had nothing in Him. John 14:30. As sin in a life increases, Satan's power over the individual increases. As the person increasingly yields to sin, Satan's hold becomes stronger and stronger until eventually it becomes so powerful that the man is absolutely helpless. He may even get to the point where his will power is completely supplanted by that of Satan or an evil spirit. In this condition he will say or do things that he never expected to do, or thought of doing, and for which he is very sorry afterwards. He may even wonder what caused him to do it. He may thru sin so yield himself to Satan that an evil spirit, instead of only influencing or periodically supplanting his will power, may literally move into that body and mind and take full possession of it, leaving the man's mind blank for a time or permanently. This condition is known as insanity or demon possession. There are also other causes for insanity but this is one of them. There is much more of this at the present time than one would suppose. So a person's yielding to sin opens the way for Satan to operate thru him and in him. The degree to which he yields determines how much of a hold Satan obtains. If he completely abandons himself to sin, then Satan's hold and bondage is complete.

The Spirit Leads This condition is paralleled in the operation of the Holy Spirit. A certain measure or degree, if those words may be used, of the Spirit is given to all believers at conversion. Whether this measure increases or decreases is determined by the man himself. There is a great contrast between the personality of Satan and that of the Holy Spirit, in that Satan forces his presence upon a person whether wanted or not, while the Spirit of God only works or comes as He is yielded to or asked. The Spirit of God in working in a life leads and suggests rather than compels. He never compels a person to do anything, while Satan does. As these suggestions and leadings are heeded they become more definite and distinct. As the person increasingly yields to them, the indwelling presence of the Spirit in that life becomes greater and greater, until at last that person lives a life completely subject to the will of God. This measure of the Spirit gives a life of victory and imparts power for larger service.

Natural Resistance Man as a free moral agent has a will of his own and this will he is very reluctant about surrendering to anyone. This natural resistance against outside influences in a way is a blessing and in another is not. It is a blessing in that it affords a natural resistance against the powers of Satan who surely would take immediate possession of every human being unless hindered from doing so. Against such intrusion the natural resistance provides a protection. If it were not there every infant would become demon possessed possibly before being born. However, it is broken down by sin, which, if continued in, eventually opens the way for the devil to do as he pleases. While this resistance is a God-given blessing and protection against undesired demonic operations, it also in turn becomes a hindrance against the desired

YIELDING TO GOD

operation of the Holy Spirit. This happens in salvation. No man can be saved against his will. So the first step must be to make him willing to yield and then after becoming willing to yield, to help him to do so. The unsaved person, being more or less in sin and as a consequence more or less robbed of the free use of his will power by the devil, finds it very difficult to make a decision for God and salvation, altho his whole being may long for it. Only God can break this power of Satan, so prayer needs to be offered for such a one. Prayer brings the power of God who breaks Satan's hold. Then the person is free to exercise his will and so becomes saved. Many for years have desired salvation but felt themselves bound, and tied and unable to say "yes," and their minds unable to act, hindered by some unseen power that would not allow them to make the desired decision. On being saved a great feeling of relief has come indicating that the will has been free of this demonic domination and has become normal.

After becoming saved, and the person is willing to allow the Lord to have His full sway, this natural resistance enters in as a mighty factor to hinder the full operation of the Spirit. The Spirit of God never forces His will on anyone but operates thru the making of suggestions, to which the will of the individual agrees; and when the individual desires and determines to do the thing suggested, the Spirit supplies the power for its accomplishment. Herein the Holy Spirit differs from the power of Satan. While the devil can, and does, force his victims to do his will and may even as in the case of demonic possession totally supplant the will and mind of the person, the Holy Spirit never compels a child of God to do His will and never supplants the will of the individual with His own. Some may question this, but let us reason together.

If the Holy Spirit supplants the will of the individual, how then could there be reward for service? We are free moral agents and there can be no reward for what we are compelled to do. So we of our own accord must be willing and then being willing it becomes our own labor. From this our own labor, with the power supplied by the power of God, God gives us a reward. Hallelujah! Our will not being supplanted by the will of the Spirit we are allowed to keep it and to do as we please and desire. Herein enters a beautiful thing. A saved person totally surrendered to God has no other desire and thought than that of pleasing Him and doing His will. So the will of God becomes incorporated into the will of the person and these both merge into one and the same thing. And the man does this will of God, not because God forced His will upon him and took away the man's will, but because the man himself makes his own thoughts and desires identical with those of the Lord. God's will becomes my will and His thoughts my thoughts, all of which is brought about by yielding to the Holy Spirit.

Our Will Supreme

For some it is far easier to yield to God than for others. To a considerable extent this is caused by natural conditions, the most common of which is a headstrong or stubborn disposition. An individual that will not readily yield to the wishes and will of other humans, will of course not readily yield to God. Many know

YIELDING TO GOD

Our
Stubborn
Will

that they are stubborn, and hate themselves for being such, but this does not necessarily make them any better. We are all more or less stubborn. We can overcome much of this by cultivating ourselves to yield and this kept up for a time may get rid of considerable of it. In attempting to surrender to God, this natural stubbornness enters in, and this, unless overcome, may become an effectual barrier against ever becoming fully yielded to the Holy Spirit. By breaking this down thru the exercise of our will power against it, and continuously and increasingly following the leadings of the Spirit, it may be removed to a large extent.

As the operations of the Spirit in a life consist primarily of leadings, He cannot successfully lead unless yielded to. Now, if a person is stubborn and self-willed, how much chance does the Spirit have of doing any leading?

Increasing
Surrender

Continually surrendering to the wishes of the Spirit brings more and more of His presence and this in turn makes His suggestions and leadings more distinct. And it is possible for this to become so pronounced that the person can live continually in the will of the Lord. Living in the will of God day and night is the secret of a happy and successful Christian experience. This increased presence of the Spirit becomes more and more felt by the person himself and by those with whom he comes in contact. A change is noticed in him. There is a victory over sin, but best of all there is power for service. If this yielding is continually prayed for and practiced, the presence and power of God may be felt in the flesh not unlike a fire. And this may culminate in the Holy Spirit's literal moving into the person and becoming a living and moving thing in his bosom.

CHAPTER X

Is the Holy Spirit a Reality?

The Spirit of God is a spirit and lives and moves in a realm of His own. He has a nature and personality such that finite beings are almost unable to grasp the mysteries of His person. Yet He is a reality.

An
Old Testament
Reality

"In the beginning God created the heavens and the earth. And the earth was waste and void; and darkness was upon the face of the deep, and the Spirit of God moved upon the face of the waters." Gen. 1:1-2. He was brooding upon the first form of God's creation and by His power thru the Word the disordered elements took their shape and form. The elements felt His presence and obeyed His will.

He was real to Enoch who "walked with God: and he was not; for God took him." Gen. 5:24. Enoch lived in His atmosphere and presence for three hundred years. This presence he not only felt but it actually operated on his body to the extent that it was changed and translated.

Old Abraham had an experience or two that showed him that the Spirit of El Shaddai—the Almighty One —was more than an influence.

The Spirit of Jehovah rested upon Moses and thru him did signs and wonders greater than those performed by Egypt's sorcerers and magicians. When the

Spirit rested upon the seventy set aside to be Moses' helpers they prophesied. They not only felt Him, but He moved upon them and their bodies were used by Him as a mouthpiece so they gave forth utterances which they had not done before and did not do again. Numbers 11:25.

"But the Spirit of Jehovah came upon Gideon." Judges 6:34. The expression in this case as well as others in the Old Testament means "clothed itself with" Gideon. Here the Spirit of God is pictured as using the man's body as a garment which implies that the man's body and faculties were at the disposal of the Spirit of God. Thus the man's body became an instrument thru which the Spirit worked and operated.

Samuel in his instruction to Saul as a preparation for his becoming king said, "After that thou shalt come to the hill of God—and thou shalt meet a band of prophets—and they will be prophesying—and the Spirit of Jehovah will come mightily upon thee, and thou shalt prophesy with them, and shalt be turned into another man." 1 Sam. 10:5-6. "And when they came thither to the hill, behold, a band of prophets met him; and the Spirit of God came mightily upon him, and he prophesied among them." 1 Sam. 10:10. Saul surely had an experience that he remembered until the time of his death and which he had not only felt upon his flesh, but which changed and fitted him for the work before him. David had a taste of this and passed thru a like experience, for, "Samuel took the horn of oil, and anointed him in the midst of his brethren: and the Spirit of Jehovah came mightily upon David from that day forward." 1 Sam. 16:13. No wonder David was the man that he was, wrote those wonderful psalms

IS THE HOLY SPIRIT A REALITY? 99

and sang those marvelous songs. Thru the revelation of the Spirit he had an insight into the deep and hidden things, and these things came forth in his writings.

And then there were the prophets of Israel, men upon whom the Spirit of Jehovah came and rested, who under the influence of the Spirit became vessels thru whom Jehovah spoke both for the time then present and for the future: who thru the Spirit could see the future things as tho they were present and whose visions have since come to pass. As Peter says, "Concerning which salvation the prophets sought and searched diligently, who prophesied of the grace that should come unto you: searching what time or what manner of time the Spirit of Christ which was in them did point unto, when it testified beforehand the sufferings of Christ, and the glories that should follow them." 1 Peter 1:10-11. The Spirit used their bodies and minds to give forth a message that they themselves were puzzled at and hardly understood, and which things the very angels desired to look into. They recognized the operation within themselves of a supernatural power and being, who possessed greater wisdom than they. And this thing was in them. Surely the Spirit was a reality to them.

When all the soothsayers and astrologers in the whole kingdom had failed, Nebuchadnezzar's dream and its interpretation was revealed to Daniel in the night. Daniel also had a heavenly visitor that for one night subjugated the ferocious nature of the hungry lions. And another whose visit came in broad daylight while he was in the king's business and in the company of many others, whose presence brought the power of God so mightily that Daniel's friends trembled and shook and ran to hide themselves while Daniel fell to the ground like one dead. Ezekiel's experience was somewhat the same for he says, "As I sat in my house, and the elders of Judah sat before me,—the hand of the Lord Jehovah fell there upon me." Ezek. 8:1. Did not Daniel and Ezekiel feel the power of God, did not their flesh experience His experience and was He not real to them?

The three Hebrews in the furnace of fire not only knew that God's power was there, but saw the definite results of His operation when He quenched the fury of the flames in protecting their clothes as well as their bodies. And the great Nebuchadnezzar and his whole army to their own astonishment and consternation became witnesses to the power of the living God.

Leaving the Old Testament we go to the New. By what power did Jesus cast out demons and raise the dead, and by what power did the apostles and disciples do the same? By what power did the lame walk, the blind see, the deaf hear, and were the maimed restored? By the finger of God and the power of the Holy Spirit.

An Early Church Reality What came upon the disciples when they were in the upper room? Did they feel it, did they experience anything, did it last, and what change came over them if any? In whose power did Peter preach so that three thousand and five thousand were saved, or did Stephen, the first martyr, confound the Jews? If God's Spirit and power was a reality in the Old Testament He was tenfold more so in the New.

And the power that inaugurated the days of grace is still here and has not changed in the least. If His presence healed the sick, raised the dead, cast out

IS THE HOLY SPIRIT A REALITY?

demons and filled men and women so they both felt it and knew it, He can and is willing to do the same now. Oh, Hallelujah! Men are well willing to concede that such things were, but hesitate to acknowledge that such things are. As long as the days of grace last and the present gospel dispensation is with us, all the promises given for it are still operative for all who will claim them. The Spirit of God is just as real now as He ever was and is just as capable of operating and manifesting Himself as at any other time in this dispensation.

Does it seem possible that such a wonderful and powerful being as the Holy Spirit who so singularly affected men in the days of old could live in a person to-day and not allow His presence to become known in some definite way? If He manifested Himself in some way when He dwelt in people years ago, will He not let it be known in some way when He lives in people to-day? Has the Spirit in these last days changed His nature so that now He is quiet and passive where He before was active and aggressive?

Self-delusion Many these days are taking the Holy Spirit "by faith." By this they mean that their asking and attempts at believing have made them possessors of Him. Feeling or no feeling, evidence or no evidence, they base their faith on the promise of the Lord in Mark 11:24: "All things whatsoever ye pray and ask for, believe that ye receive them, and ye shall have them." True, living faith can accomplish all things, but real living faith comes from God and is not manufactured in or by ourselves. Trying to make oneself believe never brings faith. If anything, it only increases the doubt. Unless there is a definite assurance from God that the request has been granted, it is ridiculous to try to believe in the actual possession of something that is not there. Many times we have heard people testifying to being healed when no healing or change had taken place and when possibly the disease culminated in death. Does God get any glory from such things? It is perfectly right to say that we believe that God shall do a thing and that we possess it by faith but not by actual possession. Such faith brings results. Anything possessed "by faith" is only distant, on the way, in the future and inoperative. We hope for it. But possession ends the hope and the thing desired becomes living, real, operative and tangible. Those who possess the Spirit "by faith" usually have little or nothing to show for their efforts. Their lives are just as empty, lean, and negative as before they took Him "by faith." Those who possess Him in reality have His living, operating presence, which shows forth in almost every action. Let no one suppose that it is unscriptural to lay claim to God's promises by faith. Far from it. But it is both unscriptural and illogical to say that we have in actual possession something that we are still exercising faith for and hoping to receive. We do not hope or exercise faith for what we already have.

A hungry, starving man takes a meal "by faith," but he smells, tastes, eats and absorbs nothing, and while taking his nourishment by this process goes on toward starvation. But when he has his meal in actual possession he smells, tastes, chews, swallows, and enjoys it while his body is strengthened by its contents. What a difference!

It   A real infilling of the Holy Spirit brings a soul-
Is   satisfaction that no one can describe and
Real   nothing can be compared with. It brings with
it a knowledge that the action took place and takes place, and that the Spirit continually abides. The possessor can definitely say, "I have Him. I know when He came in, and He now abides for I feel His presence and experience His operations."

God's power was real to those of Old Testament days and also to the early church. They knew His presence and did not have to guess it. He is and can be just as real to-day. There is such a thing as a real infilling experience and the one who receives it knows that he has the Holy Spirit and when He came in.

CHAPTER XI

Why the Power Is Necessary

Christianity arrived in the world at a time when it was badly needed. Rome, the master of the then known world, was corrupt, rotten and immoral to the core. The glory of Greece was waning and she, too, if anything, was worse than Rome in her licentious living and immorality. Egypt's star had set, but she was still the winter playground for the rich and lazy and what Rome and Greece could not supply to satisfy the desires of the flesh, she both could and did. Aside from
Demons Worshiped the Jews the whole then known world was idolatrous and demon oppressed to the extreme. The religions of Rome, Greece and Egypt were vile, unclean and degrading, and consisted of worshiping demons under the names of gods and goddesses. Their priests were obsessed and possessed with demons and in the power of these demons, masquerading as gods, they performed signs and wonders which in some instances were truly remarkable.

These religions had a powerful hold upon the superstitious people who demanded supernatural manifestations. These demonic gods were invoked upon all occasions of importance. The entrails of sacrificed fowls and animals were closely examined for signs and marks. Flights of migrating birds were noted, the direction of the winds, condition of the clouds, phases of the moon

WHY THE POWER IS NECESSARY 105

and stars and the actions of animals. The statues and monuments of men and gods were reported both to move and speak.

The formation of condensed water vapor, or sweating, upon a vessel containing water was considered an ill omen, and if upon a statue or an image was a sure sign of divine wrath and calamity. To such people ghosts were invariably real.

Before Julius Caesar crossed the river Rubicon to enter Italy and fight against Pompey and eventually become the ruler of the whole Roman empire, his soothsayers killed the sacrificial birds and read the signs. During the Carthaginian War when the presence of the terrible Hannibal's army threatened the very life of the republic, a certain Roman general for weeks hesitated to attack because the signs were against him.

In Rome were the Sibylline books containing warnings and prophecies given under the divine inspiration of the gods. In these the emperor as the Pontifex Maximus or high priest of the nation sought advice and information in times of national danger or calamity.

In Egypt, a female deity, the goddess Isis, was worshiped. Her devotees, by certain secret incantations, could call forth demons of different names, who were able to perform certain cures and heal certain diseases. These demons were very powerful and evidently of greater strength than those which caused the diseases. They were therefore able to bind and remove the influence of these lesser ones. Satan was willing to lose a body in order to gain a soul. These priests of Isis at times became obsessed of demon power and while under this influence could tell what was going on at a distance and would also rave and prophesy.

Scattered over the then known world were various shrines and temples, possibly the most notable of which was the Temple of the goddess Diana at Ephesus, in which city Paul preached and the power of the Spirit of God worked so mightily. Images of this goddess, when worshiped were supposed to bring notable benefits especially to mothers.

At Delphi was the great oracle to the god Apollo. Over a crevice in the rocks, out of which issued poisonous vapors, stood a temple. Seated on a chair over this crevice, and in these rooms, the devotees would become stupified by the vapors. While in this condition the demon or demons professing to be the god Apollo would enter into the body of the person, often causing swelling of the abdomen and violent heavings of the chest. Then using the vocal organs of the person he would cause him to rave and prophesy and often tell of things going on at a distance. Sometimes they would see visions or be in a trance. At times ignorant persons while under this influence would speak on subjects with which they were in no way acquainted and even compose poetry and literature which were masterpieces of refinement and rhetoric. At times in other oracles and shrines drugged wine was used to produce this stupor. This is what Paul had in mind when he spoke about the cup of the Lord and the cup of the demons.

A ruler of these days wished to test the individual merits of several of these oracles. Choosing several trusted servants, he sent them to Delphi with the instructions to arrive at a certain time, and at that time ask what their master was doing at that moment. On the day set the men arrived, but before they ever had a chance to tell their errand a prophetess approached and told them what their errand was and just what the king was doing at that time. All of which was correct to the letter.

Tremendous Opposition Met Into a world in this condition Christianity arrived, and against these religions, superstitions and demonic powers it had to battle to survive and conquer. It becomes very evident that no man-made religion or cunningly devised fables ever would make any headway against such odds. It takes power to overcome power and the stronger overcomes. God did not leave His church powerless and at the mercy of these terrible resisting forces, but thru the Holy Spirit supplied all that she needed. Jesus Himself had said, "But ye shall receive power when the Holy Spirit is come upon you,"

Power Given which promise was literally fulfilled. The One that was in them was greater than the one that was in the world. So with the advent of Christianity a terrific battle ensued between the old and the new, between the strong which already was there, and the stronger which had just arrived, between the power of God and the power of Satan. Satan never has been able to stand in a fair contest or open battle against the power of God. So in this instance as in all others, he had to resort to underhand methods, and operating thru the then corrupt, and by himself controlled, Roman government, he sent persecution, wave upon wave of which swept over the new religion's adherents threatening again and again to blot out every vestige and remnant. But in every instance and everywhere the new order came in contact with the old, the old had to give way. The strong was conquered by the stronger. And the new order spread at first with lightning rapidity and later more gradually over the whole then known world, overthrowing the age-long superstitions of demon worship and demon theology, changing the lives of individuals, of families and eventually of whole nations. The light shone in the darkness but the darkness overcame it not. If Christianity had not arrived when it did the present history of the world could never have been written.

When the message of salvation came to a place, the present and operating power of the devil would do everything possible to keep it from getting a foothold. And at times it became a pitched battle, often lasting for considerable periods and with varying success, until at last the Lord had His own way. The Scriptures record several of these battles.

"And it came to pass, as we were going to the place of prayer, that a certain maid having a spirit of divination met us, who brought her master much gain by soothsaying: The same following after Paul and us cried out, saying, These men are servants of the Most High God, which proclaim unto you the way of salvation. And this she did for many days. But Paul, being sore troubled, turned and said to the spirit, I charge thee in the name of Jesus Christ to come out of her. And it came out that very hour." Acts 16:16-18. The unclean spirit or demon known as Python or soothsaying spirit, by reason of its great and superior wisdom, knew Paul and his followers, and speaking thru the young woman proclaimed it, as no doubt it had proclaimed many other things before and by reason of which she was of gain to her masters. Paul, by the power of God and in the name of Jesus, commanded the demon to come out, and because the power of God was stronger than the demon he had to do so, and the poor girl became normal. "But when her masters saw that the hope of their gain was gone, they laid hold on Paul and Silas, and dragged them into the market-place before the rulers."

Word Confirmed With Signs Following After the death of Stephen, Philip went down to Samaria and "proclaimed unto them the Christ. And the multitudes gave heed with one accord unto the things that were spoken by Philip, when they heard, and saw the signs which he did. For from many of those that had unclean spirits, they came out, crying with a loud voice: and many that were palsied, and that were lame, were healed." Acts 8:5-7. Here again, the conflict is pictured. These demons inhabiting the Samaritans met one of greater power and stronger than themselves and had to give way. They objected strenuously and with a loud voice to being driven out of their inhabitations, but to no avail; the conqueror had come.

"But there was a certain man, Simon by name, who beforetime in the city used sorcery, and amazed the people of Samaria, giving out that himself was some great one: to whom they all gave heed, from the least to the greatest, saying, This man is that power of God which is called Great. And they gave heed to him, because that of long time he had amazed them with his sorceries. But when they believed Philip preaching good tidings concerning the kingdom of God and the name of Jesus Christ, they were baptized, both men and women. And Simon also himself believed: and being baptized, he continued with Philip; and beholding signs and great miracles wrought, he was amazed." Acts 8:9-13. Here an apostle of each order came in direct contact and opposition. For some time Satan had had things his own way in Samaria. Thru Simon, his apostle, he had performed signs and wrought miracles that caused wonderment and this he let it be known was by the power of God. It might be noted that it is remarkable how the devil with his operations always desires to masquerade under the name of God. Possibly he desires to be a god and dethrone Jehovah Himself. But along came Philip, who in the name of Jesus Christ performed signs and wonders even greater than those of Simon. The people quickly recognized that in this new name lay greater power and authority than in any Simon may have used. So turning from Simon they believed Philip "when they heard, and saw the signs which he did." Satan had done his best to keep his hold on the people, but lost it when a greater than he—the power of God, arrived on the scene. So thru the operations and manifestations of the Spirit, attention was attracted to the name of Jesus and Philip's message, to which "the multitudes gave heed with one accord." Apparently the sorcerer himself was convinced that this thing which Philip had was greater than what he himself possessed, for "Simon also himself believed." Not only did he believe but he also desired this same power and hoped to buy it with money. What a marvelous evidence to the crushing defeat of Satan's authority.

And at Ephesus "God wrought special miracles by the hands of Paul: insomuch that unto the sick were carried away from his body, handkerchiefs or aprons, and the diseases departed from them, and the evil spirits went out. But certain also of the strolling Jews, exorcists, took upon them to name over them that had the evil spirits the name of the Lord Jesus, saying, I adjure you by Jesus whom Paul preacheth. And there were seven sons of one Sceva, a Jew, a chief priest, who did this. And the evil spirit answered and said unto them, Jesus I know (or recognize), and Paul I know; but who are ye? And the man in whom the evil spirit was leaped on them, and mastered both of them, and prevailed against them, so that they fled out of that house naked and wounded. And this became known to all, both Jews and Greeks, that dwelt at Ephesus; and fear fell upon them all, and the name of the Lord Jesus was magnified. Many also of them that had believed came, confessing, and declaring their deeds. And not a few of them that practiced magical arts brought their books together, and burned them in the sight of all; and they counted the price of them, and found it fifty thousand pieces of silver. So mightily grew the word of the Lord and prevailed." Acts 19:11-20.

Here, as it were, Paul bearded the lion in his den. This city contained the temple of the goddess Diana whose worship filled all Asia Minor. In the city and the surrounding country were thousands of her devotees. Sorcery, witchcraft and other things of demonical nature were universally practiced.

Special Anointing — To successfully fight this the Lord clothed him with a special anointing, the results of which the record shows. But it was not Paul who did these things. It was the power of the

Holy Spirit and he was but a channel thru whom He operated.

The incident of the strolling Jews is unique in that it showed that the demons recognized the authority of Jesus and knew Paul. But they refused in any way to submit to these others, or to any of less power than themselves, and quickly showed their displeasure at being disturbed by venting their wrath upon the bodies of these Jews, much to the Jews' discomfort and consternation. We can rest assured that these sons of Sceva did not try that trick again. Thru this it became evident that the name of Jesus was not to be trifled with and that Paul's ministry had greater power than those who practiced witchcraft and sorcery. It also showed the sorcerers and practicers of witchcraft how powerless their own efforts were against the powers of evil, and becoming frightened they confessed and burned their books.

"So they, being sent forth by the Holy Spirit, went down to Seleucia; and from thence they sailed to Cyprus. And when they were at Salamis, they proclaimed the word of God in the synagogues of the Jews: and they had also John as their attendant. And when they had gone thru the whole island unto Paphos, they found a certain sorcerer, a false prophet, a Jew, whose name was Bar-Jesus; who was with the proconsul, Sergius Paulus, a man of understanding. The same called unto him Barnabas and Saul, and sought to hear the word of God. But Elymas the sorcerer (for so is his name by interpretation) withstood them, seeking to turn aside the proconsul from the faith. But Saul, who is also called Paul, filled with the Holy Spirit, fastened his eyes on him, and said, O full of all guile and all villainy, thou son of the devil, thou enemy of all righteousness, wilt thou not cease to pervert the right ways of the Lord? And now, behold, the hand of the Lord is upon thee, and thou shalt be blind, not seeing the sun for a season. And immediately there fell on him a mist and a darkness; and he went about seeking some to lead him by the hand. Then the proconsul, when he saw what was done, believed, being astonished at the teaching of the Lord." Acts 13:4-12.

How the devil does try to keep the word of truth away from hungry people! The proconsul was open for an honest conviction, but the sorcerer, filled with hell itself, withstood and tried to prevent it. But the Spirit of God in Paul rebuking him, called him by his right name and told the nature of his activities. On top of it all the Holy Spirit showed His mastery over the power of Satan by bringing physical discomfort upon the sorcerer, which Satan could in nowise prevent. This the proconsul saw and in it recognized the value of the gospel that Paul was preaching, being astonished at the teaching of the Lord.

We might go on telling of how when shipwrecked, Paul being bitten by a viper shook it off into the fire and suffered no hurt, this opening the way for Paul's ministry among the people there. Or of Peter and John's healing of the lame man sitting at the gate Beautiful in the temple, which healing drew thousands together and opened their minds to hear and receive Peter's preaching, which resulted in the conversion of some five thousand souls in one day. Or how Peter at Joppa thru the power of the Spirit raised up Dorcas from the dead, which miracle paved the way for a continued stay in that place. But these are sufficient to show that thru the operations of God's Spirit in healing the sick, casting out demons and the like, the Lord proved that the gospel and the name of Jesus was of greater power and of more value than that of the false religions of the day.

When Paul was at Corinth his speech and preaching "were not in the persuasive words of wisdom, but in the demonstration of the Spirit and of power." So it was the indwelling and operating presence of the Holy Spirit in the disciples that accomplished these things. And Paul overcame the wisdom, knowledge and arguments of the Greek philosophers, not because he was any wiser or more learned than they, but because the Holy Spirit demonstrated and operated. This became a living and tangible proof of the reality of God. So this indwelling presence of the Spirit endued the individual with gifts and these gifts produced manifestations of various kinds, which manifestations attracted the attention of the people to the man, to his message, and especially to Jesus in whose name they were done. As these manifestations were greater, and more powerful and beneficial than those of their former gods and goddesses they naturally turned to the Lord.

Nothing short of this demonstration of the Spirit and power could have made Christianity a success and it was this which made it a conquering force which everywhere overthrew the power and strongholds of the devil and gave the converts strength to stand. Without it the preaching of the gospel would have been a farce and a futile effort.

The Promise Fulfilled The Lord had promised: "And these signs shall accompany them that believe: in my name shall they cast out demons; they shall speak with new tongues; they shall take up serpents, and if they drink any deadly thing, it shall in no wise hurt them; they shall lay hands on the sick, and they shall recover." Mark 16:17-18. And it was the fulfillment of this which gave Christianity its vital force and made it a conquering agent rather than a dead religion. The priest of the Egyptian goddess Isis performed his miracles in the name of Isis his god. The priest of Apollo did his signs, wonders and soothsaying in the name of Apollo, the god or goddess in each instance receiving the credit for the act. Likewise, the believer in Christ performed his miracles, powers and healings in the name of his God, Jesus of Nazareth, and Jesus received credit for the thing done. By comparing the signs and wonders accomplished, the onlooking world soon saw which god was the stronger. It was this comparison which proved that Jesus was not a dead man buried in a tomb but a living, powerful Deity greater than all the gods and goddesses of Greece, Rome and Egypt. As a result, the word of God grew and prospered.

God's Power Necessary To-day Christianity to-day is just as badly in need of the power of God and the presence and operation of the Holy Spirit as in the days of the early church. Because of this lack of power it is gradually losing its hold upon the masses. Not that the gospel has changed in the least, but rather because men are presenting only a small portion of it, that portion which agrees with their little brains and understanding. The supernatural is being left out as unreasonable and impossible. If the supernatural is left out of Christianity it becomes of no more effect than any of the other religions and in some cases less so. It is the supernatural that the people are looking for and have a reason to expect. God is a supernatural God and should He not work in a supernatural way? Conviction of sin, conversion and power over evil habits are all supernatural phenomena. In the early days, demons masquerading as gods and goddesses performed the supernatural and therefore captivated the minds of the people. But when the Lord thru the Holy Spirit performed even greater supernatural things they saw that He was the mightier, therefore more worthy of their affection, worship and allegiance.

God Not Changed — Why should not the supernatural operate to-day? Has God changed? Is His Spirit less mighty? Is it not needed? The various cults of this time, which are but the same demon religions of long ago that have come back under a new name and adjusted to to-day's conditions, are performing signs and wonders thru their mental and magnetic healings and various spirit manifestations. By this means they are getting as their followers some of the best people of the country, all because they produce something supernatural, something tangible which a thinking mind can see and hear. Why should not Christianity produce that which is supernatural, thru the operating of the Holy Spirit, which would afford the same or greater tangible evidence of the existence of the real and living God? Why allow Satan to continue his lying, soul-destroying operations un-

WHY THE POWER IS NECESSARY

challenged all the while claiming that these things are of God, and not allow Jehovah Himself a chance to prove His own identity and power? But how can He when the professed Christians are not filled with His Spirit and when the gifts and manifestations are explained as belonging to another age or time, or are even called of the devil?

For Us Also

Unless there is a return of the supernatural in Christianity, which in turn means no more nor less than a return of the power of the Spirit into the saints, the natural result and consequence will be a gradual decay which even now is going on.

Oh, for the old-time power of God, the true gifts and manifestations of the Spirit and Spirit-filled men and women endued with power from on high that the world may see that Jehovah of Hosts, the God of Israel, still lives and has power over sin, hell, flesh and the devil. We are just as badly in need of the fulfillment of the Lord's promise to the disciples in Mark 16:17 as they of the early church.

CHAPTER XII

This Is That

In Acts 1:5, Luke records Jesus as telling the expectant disciples just before His ascension, "Ye shall be baptized in the Holy Spirit not many days hence." The full import of these words never dawned upon them until later. But, nevertheless, they already had some experience and knowledge concerning the power of God. Twelve at one time and seventy at another had been sent forth on gospel tours, in which they mightily proclaimed that the kingdom of heaven was at hand. By the "finger of God" they had healed the sick and cast out demons. They had come back rejoicing and glad because the power of the Spirit operated thru them to the extent of rebuking evil spirits who became subject unto them in the name of Jesus. When Jesus was accused by the Jews of casting out demons by Beelzebub, the prince of demons, He told them plainly that it was by the finger of God and the power of the Spirit that it was done. And then He asked, "And by whom do your sons cast them out?" implying that it was by the same power of the Spirit of God.

Shall Be in You   Jesus was endeavoring to prepare them for the coming event. On that memorable night just before His crucifixion the disciples crowded around Him to absorb His every word of advice and admonition. They were told concerning the Spirit, "Ye know him; for he abideth with you, and shall be in you." The Holy Spirit was no stranger to them; for He abode with them. But a new experience was coming. He was to be in them, something evi-dently deeper and different. No doubt their minds reasoned after this fashion: "What can this mean, to be baptized in the Spirit? What will it feel like and what will happen? How shall we know when it takes place and what will be the results upon us? We are already saved for our names are written in heaven, but what will this new experience be like?"

They did not have to wait long. Tarrying for a few days brought the promise of the Father upon them, for "When the day of Pentecost was now come, they were all together in one place. And suddenly there came from heaven a sound as of the rushing of a mighty wind, and it filled all the house where they were sitting. And there appeared unto them tongues parting asunder, like as of fire; and it sat upon each one of them. And they were all filled with the Holy Spirit, and began to speak with other tongues, as the Spirit gave them utterance." Acts 2:1-4.

What had happened? The baptism of the Holy Spirit that Jesus a few days before had promised had taken place. "And when this sound was heard, the multitude came together, and were confounded." Acts 2:6. There surely was some excitement in Jerusalem that morning. "And they were all amazed and marvelled." Little wonder, for here was a new *Joel's* thing. "And they were all amazed, and *Prophecy* were perplexed, saying one to another, What meaneth this?" To their question

Peter answered, "Ye men of Judea, and all ye that dwell at Jerusalem, be this known unto you, and give ear unto my words. For these are not drunken, as ye suppose,—but this is that which hath been spoken thru the prophet Joel;

"And it shall be in the last days, saith God, I will pour forth of my Spirit upon all flesh: and your sons and your daughters shall prophesy, and your young men shall see visions, and your old men shall dream dreams: Yea and on my servants and on my handmaidens in those days will I pour forth of my Spirit; and they shall prophesy."

Jesus had instructed them to wait for the promise of the Father. This promise the Father had given thru the prophet Joel hundreds of years before. Peter told his audience that the experience that they had just gone thru was the fulfillment of what Joel had prophesied and Jesus had verified. Peter surely knew what he was talking about. Could a man so recently baptized with the Spirit and who at that moment was being thrilled in his very flesh by His presence get up before these people and tell them something which was not true? Does any man dare say that Peter was mistaken? Who is that man and where does he stand in the councils of God and what measure of the Spirit rests on him? Peter filled with the Spirit knew more of God and was more in position to speak of the things of God than all the Spiritless men of education before his time and since. "Oh foolish men, and slow of heart to believe in all that the prophets have spoken."

"Now when they heard this, they were pricked in their heart, and said unto Peter and the rest of the apostles, Brethren, what shall we do? And Peter said unto them, Repent ye, and be baptized every one of you in the name of Jesus Christ unto the remission of your sins; and ye shall receive the gift of the Holy Spirit. For to you is the promise, and to your children, and to all that are afar off, even as many as the Lord our God shall call unto Him." Acts 2:37-39. Was this promise of the Father for these one hundred and twenty only? Peter said, "It is unto you"—meaning thereby his whole audience and these were three thousand or more. It was also for their children, both living and unborn. This extended the promise at least another generation or possibly more, and increased the number by thousands. He added that it is also to them that were afar off, which included the Jews of the dispersion scattered in Italy, Greece, Egypt, Babylon and dozens of other places. And last of all, it was "to as many as the Lord our God shall call unto Him," giving no limit as to number, time, place or race. This included the Gentiles also, for they later received the very self-same experience. So the promise given by the Father thru Joel, and restated and fortified by Jesus, is for as many as the Lord shall call unto Himself, which means nothing more or less than all those who have been drawn to the Lord thru the Holy Spirit and who have accepted salvation. What a bountiful God and wonderful gift!

Unto All That Are Afar Off

When Peter tells them, "And ye shall receive the gift of the Holy Spirit," just what has he in mind? Does he mean that they shall have that abiding presence which the disciples had possessed when they walked with Jesus? Or does he mean that same experience of being filled and baptized such as they had just gone thru?

Notice that Peter says that the baptism which the apostles had just received was the fulfillment of Joel's prophecy and that this same prophecy is for these others also. By this he tries to convey to them the thought and idea that they who believed and were baptized were candidates for the identical baptism which the apostles themselves had received. And such it was, as evidenced from the Word and history. Years later, when Paul was at Ephesus the same imparting of the Spirit was given to those twelve disciples who previously had been baptized unto John's baptism. Many Bible students and commentators are emphatic in believing that this is also what happened to Philip's converts at Samaria, for as Peter and John laid their hands upon them after praying, the Holy Spirit came upon them. It is very evident that this was accompanied by some visible and audible phenomenon as Simon the sorcerer wished to buy with money the same power that the apostles had so that when he laid hands on people the same thing would happen. Church history clearly records that for at least the first three centuries or until A. D. 330 and later the same apostolic infilling of the Spirit was imparted to the greatest majority of the believers. In

Early Church Days

fact, before a candidate was immersed in water, prayer was offered that the Spirit might be given at baptism and in most cases the Spirit fell upon the person while in the water or shortly afterwards. At other times special times of prayer and fasting were set aside for those who were to be, or had been, baptized in water that the Spirit might come upon them, with the result that almost invariably He did fall upon them. And this falling of the Spirit was almost without exception accompanied by the same manifestations as came upon the apostles on the day of Pentecost. This clearly shows that the promise of the Father thru Joel was in operation for several hundred years after the initial visitation. And why should it not be? Was not the promise unto "all that the Lord our God shall call unto Him"?

When the Roman government officially adopted Christianity, all persecution ceased and a lukewarmness set in which quenched the Spirit, but, nevertheless, the same baptism, altho quite uncommon, has here and there in history showed forth and at last even come down to our day. It is evident that the promise is for the whole Gentile age rather than just a portion of it. And if it is for the whole age it is for us now. We have as much right to its fulfillment as any of the saints of this age. If it is not for us, then how can we account for the innumerable cases in which saints at widely separated points, among various races and at different times over the whole earth are receiving this same experience which the apostles received?

It was contrary to Jewish custom for an orthodox Jew to enter into the home or eat with an uncircumcised Gentile. Any Jew considered doing so a breach of etiquette and even sin. But God thru the Spirit in a vision over-ruled this, so Peter, taking six men with him who were also of the circumcision, journeyed to Caesarea and entered into the home of one Cornelius,

Cornelius'
Household

an officer in the Roman army, a centurion, of the cohort called the Italian band, who was a devout man, and one that feared God with all his house, who gave much alms to the people, and prayed to God alway. Acts 10.

This Cornelius had been visited by an angel who had told him to send for Peter. And when Peter came he found them all waiting and ready to "hear all things that have been commanded thee of the Lord."

So Peter opened his mouth and preached Christ unto them. He did not say one word about the baptism of the Spirit or of his own experience on the day of Pentecost. Nevertheless, "while Peter yet spake these words, the Holy Spirit fell on all them that heard the word. And they of the circumcision that believed were amazed, as many as came with Peter, because that on the Gentiles also was poured out the gift of the Holy Spirit." And they knew that the Spirit had come upon them "for they heard them speak with tongues, and magnify God."

"Now the apostles and the brethren that were in Judea heard that the Gentiles also had received the word of God. And when Peter was come up to Jerusalem, they that were of the circumcision contended with him, saying, Thou wentest in to men uncircumcised; and didst eat with them." Acts 11:1-3. In the eyes of these people Peter had broken the tradition of the fathers and had committed sin. And even tho he was considered as one of the chief apostles he was severely taken to task for what he had done. These with whom he now dealt were not ignorant but men zealous for God and not easily dissuaded from their ideas and beliefs. Peter's excuses and reasons for his conduct would have to be sound and scriptural or they would be torn to a thousand pieces. There Peter stood before the council at Jerusalem to answer for his doings.

So he started in by telling them of his own vision and that of Cornelius and ended by saying, "And as I began to speak, the Holy Spirit fell on them, even as on us at the beginning. And I remembered the word of the Lord, how that He said, John indeed baptized with water; but ye shall be baptized in the Holy Spirit. If then God gave unto them the like gift as he did also unto us . . . " Acts 11:15-17. Here Peter definitely stated that the Gentiles had received the same gift as the apostles themselves had received and called it the baptism of the Holy Spirit.

The Evidence What became the evidence to the gathered council that the Spirit had come upon the Gentiles? If in answer to some one's question, "Peter, how did you know that the Holy Spirit came upon them?" he had said, "Several of them shook very violently," would they have been satisfied? What if he had made the statement, "Many fell prostrate upon the floor for a long time and others screamed at the top of their voices," would they have agreed to this, saying, "Yes, Peter, that is a certain evidence that they were baptized in the Holy Spirit"? Or suppose he had replied, "They all clapped their hands and jumped up and down and sang and shouted, while others sat very still and quiet as a feeling of great peace came over them," would such answers or evidence have satisfied this highly critical audience so that when they heard these things they held their peace, and glorified God? Never! They wanted more substantial evidence than such. Yet thousands to-day believe and are being told that going thru such performances and receiving such blessings and anointings are genuine proof of having received the baptism of the Holy Spirit.

On what grounds did Peter say, "The Holy Spirit

fell on them, even as on us at the beginning," and "God gave unto them the like gift as he did also unto us"? Because he "heard them speak with tongues, and magnify God." In other words, the same phenomenon had taken place upon the Gentiles and they had received the same experience as the apostles did at the beginning, and this Peter called the baptism of the Holy Spirit. Peter gauged their experience by his own. When he received the baptism certain things happened to him and when he saw the same things happen to these Gentiles he knew that the same baptism had come to them. And this speaking in an unknown language under the ecstasy of the Spirit, and prophecy, became the infallible proof to the assembled council that God had given to the Gentiles the same salvation and Holy Spirit as He had to the Jews.

Let us thank God for all that we receive, much of the Spirit or little, but why not press on and take all that He has to give? If the prophecy of Joel gives the promise to us, why be satisfied with any less than the fullest measure of it? God never gives anything unless it is needed. And this fullness and baptism of the Spirit is promised and given because His saints in this age, and especially now, need all that they can possess. Why be so negligent toward ourselves as to hesitate to make use of what God so freely offers to all who ask? What God has provided He desires that we make use of and let us not be satisfied with any less than the best He has.

CHAPTER XIII

The Infilling and Its Evidence

"Well," some one says, "if a person can be both saved and have the Spirit before being baptized or filled with the Spirit, what is the use of pressing on and getting any more? And how does a person know when he is filled?"

Not a Plaything — Let it be emphatically stated that God never gives anything to His children simply that they may have a good feeling or a new plaything. Every gift of God is for a specific purpose and to supply a specific need. So we can rest assured that if God has the full apostolic baptism to give and does give it, it is not in order to supply a new set of feelings and sensations. Nor is it because those to whom it is given are special pets and privileged characters, but rather because this apostolic baptism and what it brings is needed in this day and age, both in the individual and in the church as a whole. So the possession of the full measure of the Spirit is not only a privilege but also a necessity.

The More The Better — Altho the partial infilling and abiding presence of the Spirit are good, each increase of the presence of the Spirit in the life is just that much better, and the full indwelling presence best of all. Our degree of Christianity is directly dependent upon the degree of the presence of Christ in our lives. The more of Christ we have, the more we are like Him and the more the world can see His image in us. Paul speaks of "Christ in you, the hope of glory," and also of having "this treasure in earthen vessels." It is this "Christ in us" that makes us Christians and children of God. It is this which differentiates us from the world and the children of the devil, and gives us victory over sin, hell, flesh and the things of Satan. In the greater measure that we have Christ in us and that He is allowed to reign and rule in our hearts, the greater is our separation from the world, the more the fruits of the Spirit in our lives, the more we are ready and awaiting the coming of the Lord, the greater our enjoyment of salvation, and the greater the extent and power of our service.

But "Christ in us" is only revealed thru the Holy Spirit, and it is His specific work and calling to develop and unfold this "Christ in us" which is given to all true believers. A partial presence of the Spirit in the life will give a partial revelation of Christ. The greater the presence of the Spirit the more possible it is for Him to do His work and bring this revelation. Our salvation consists of nothing more or less than the revelation of Christ and His operating in us. So the degree of our salvation, if we may use that term, is both directly and indirectly dependent upon the degree of the presence of the Spirit. Therefore the degree of our possessing the Holy Spirit is of vital importance.

Infilling Is of Value The full infilling becomes of value in that it brings a practically boundless presence of Spirit into our lives, the Spirit's operations becoming limited only by the person's mental and physical ability to receive. A smaller mental capacity can grasp less than a larger one. A mind like that of Paul or Isaiah was far more capable of taking hold of and handling the truths revealed by the Spirit than one of lesser development.

The full infilling is also of great value in that it cannot take place until a person is fully yielded to the will of God. And this full yieldedness to the will of God puts a person in position where God can trust him with the deeper things and with greater power without much danger of his becoming conceited over the possession of them.

So the question becomes one of how to truly yield so that the Spirit of God may take full possession. One peculiar thing about the nature of the Holy Spirit is that in all His dealings with God's people He is very mild and gentle in all His actions and forces His will on no one. He leads, but does not compel or force. Jesus says of Him, "He shall guide you into all the truth," and Paul says, "They that are led by the Spirit are sons of God."

Yielding Necessary In His brooding over and around a person for the purpose of eventually taking up His complete abode, He only takes possession as possession is granted. He never goes further than He is asked to go, or that it is desired that He should go. Any one can limit His presence or blessing by saying, "Stay thy hand, Lord." He stops right there and never goes any further or deeper until asked to do so. So the person himself paves the way and also determines his own blessing by how much room he gives to the Spirit. The more room he gives, the more the

Spirit moves in. The more he yields and surrenders, the more the Spirit takes possession.

Now, the Spirit of God, altho a person, is also a power. And this power can be felt upon the flesh and is as real as an electric current, and produces a very pleasant sensation as it passes thru the body or rests upon it. Many people seek the power of God for no other reason than to enjoy the pleasant sensations that this power brings. The sensations are the least part of the blessings.

The Flesh Resists It is a natural tendency for the body to resist exterior influence of whatever nature it may be. For instance, many persons put up a terrific struggle when going under an anesthetic. They cannot bear the thought of giving up consciousness. It is a known fact that very few persons can be hypnotized against their will. Such as deal with familiar spirits, spiritualistic mediums, find that they must cultivate yielding to these demonic forces often for years before they can place themselves under the control of these devilish influences. This resistance and inability to yield also extends to the Holy Spirit. Just why a person that is saved and really loves the Lord should hesitate or dread to yield to what he knows is the Spirit of God is hard to say, but nevertheless such all too often happens to be the case. This resistance is often independent of the person's will. The mind will say, "Yes, Lord, have Thy way," while the flesh will oppose with might and main.

In our flesh lies the seat of all that is evil within us, and thru this avenue comes all our temptations. "The mind of the flesh is enmity against God; for it is not

THE INFILLING AND ITS EVIDENCE 131

subject to the law of God." Before the Holy Spirit can take up His full abode in a person this flesh must be put in a position and condition such that He can do so. Many anointings and temporary fillings can and may come before the fullness of the power arrives. But these are all smaller and in a way different from the great fullness that arrives at the baptism.

No Two Alike The process of being filled with the Spirit and the incidents leading to it differ with different persons, dependent upon their own personal make-up and in a measure upon conditions surrounding them. With some, the power of the Spirit may come with the rushing of a mighty wind, as it were, and in a few moments the work is done. This takes place when those who are candidates are ready and ripe for it, such as the disciples on the day of Pentecost and those of Cornelius' household. This also happened twice in the early eighteenth century to large gatherings of Moravians, who after periods of prayer and fasting presented themselves to God. It also happens now at times to individuals. But in the majority of cases it is more of a gradual process. The Spirit of God will often come upon a person again and again with an intervening time of days, and even weeks, before the final fullness arrives.

Obstacles It is surprising how much undesirable material there is in the average child of God that must be removed before the Spirit can fully take possession. Among these things are pride, conceit, stubbornness, and related things of the flesh. In the course of these preliminary visits of the Spirit these things are pointed out. If they are held on to by the person, the work of the Spirit stops right there and does not proceed until they are removed. If the person refuses to have them removed the operation of the Spirit totally ceases and the person goes back into his original condition or one much worse. But if the person is honest and willing, the work of the Spirit proceeds until all the obstacles are gone, and then He moves in for a permanent abode. A person newly saved usually receives the fullness very quickly if it is asked for. It seems as tho that great wonderful washing in the blood of Christ which forgives sins and ushers in salvation effectually paves the way for the immediate entrance of the fullness of the Spirit. If the power of God is mightily present and the person knows enough to ask for it, quite often the process of being saved and filled with the Spirit takes place at the same time. This produces very powerful conversions.

Demon Opposition Some people are inhabited by a demon, or demons, of which they may or may not be ignorant. If such is the case this demon must be removed before the Spirit can move in. Demonic possession or obsession in most, if not all cases, exists because of the presence of some underlying sin. Unless this sin is given up and surrendered the demon cannot be forced out. If the sin is surrendered, the Spirit of God binds and casts out this demon. At times the demon, while being cast out, protests very violently both by physical action and violent contortions, and in some instances with vocal utterances and words of blasphemy and curses. These actions are very unseemly and disgusting, and are by some mistaken for the manifestations of the power of God.

Here is where the operation of the gift of discernment is to a great advantage. Many leaders have failed to recognize these demon ravings as such. The demon obsessed individual, instead of being delivered, has continued in this state with worse results upon himself and terrible consequences upon the congregation.

Complete Surrender   With the way cleared and the obstacles removed, the Spirit moves in. But before He takes full possession the whole body must be yielded to Him. This includes every portion, nerve, fiber, muscle, and so forth, from the top of the head to the soles of the feet. To bring about this subjection the power of God will operate gently, sweetly, beautifully upon the flesh. At first the flesh will rebel and resist, and this resistance will often produce muscular movements, such as gentle movements of the limbs and a trembling thru the whole being. As the yielding progresses and increases these movements become less and less. When the yieldedness is complete they totally cease, and a deep stillness and quietness comes. The power of the Spirit can be felt burning like a mighty fire in the very bones, and filling the whole body with a something that feels like a powerful electric current passing thru the whole frame. If others are near by they sense a feeling of holiness and sanctity and the power of God that brings an atmosphere of heaven in a way that is beyond the ability of words to describe. Sometimes others touching the body or clothes of the one being filled will receive a distinct shock.

The Spirit Speaks — These preliminary broodings of the Spirit are for the purpose of assuming full mastery of that person and of subjecting the whole body to His will. This operating and subjecting process even includes the vocal organs. But singularly enough, this is most often left to the very last, until all the rest of the body has become completely subjected. Possibly there is a reason for this. We know both from experience and from the word of God that our tongue is the most difficult part of ourselves to overcome and to master. Evidently the Holy Spirit, in His operation, finds that the tongue is the most difficult, and therefore the last of all for Him to conquer. Sometimes the vocal organs are not affected until all other things are out of the way. Sometimes they are played upon as others are being finished. In some cases the Spirit takes complete control in an instant and without any preliminary activities, but usually, like the others, it is a more gradual process. As the yielding increases His mastery increases, commencing first with a few inarticulate utterances often repeated, and then developing into words and later sentences. Invariably these words and sentences are in some language unknown to the person himself, and consist of words and statements of praise and worship and adoration to God. At times they may be prophetic statements, or even become a sermon or an exhortation to repentance. Sometimes as much as half a dozen or more languages may be used. But in all instances they concern themselves with the work of the Lord and never deal with profane or common things. It is often the case that altho the person himself does not know what he is saying, only knowing that he is under the influence of some supernatural power which feels very beautiful upon his flesh, that others who may hear this may thoroly understand the language being spoken. At times, just as the Spirit has taken complete charge, the person will have visions of the Lord or be in a trance. It is very seldom that consciousness is lost. At all times he knows what is going on and knows that it is the power of God that is upon him and not some other influence.

The Value of Tongues These utterances in the unknown tongue are of no great general value except as they are of personal blessing to the individual and evidence a near and powerful presence of God. However, as an evidence that the complete infilling of the Spirit has arrived they cannot be rated too highly. The Spirit never speaks forth thru a person clearly until the whole being is under His domination and the one hundred per cent surrender has taken place. This condition arrived at, the Spirit literally moves in and takes up His abode in that person's very body, fulfilling the words of Jesus, "From within him shall flow rivers of living water," and "this," says John, "spake He of the Spirit, which they that believed on Him were to receive: for the Spirit was not yet given." When this takes place the Spirit remains with the individual continuously. This differs materially from the occasional visits and anointings that may and do take place with lesser experiences.

So the speaking in the unknown language, altho of very little value as a gift, becomes of extreme importance as the evidence that the complete surrender has taken place and that the fullness of the Spirit has come to abide. In fact, no matter how great may have been the blessings and anointings and presence of the Spirit previously, when this takes place it brings a power of the Spirit into the life that exceeds all others manyfold.

Possibly there is another reason why the speaking in an unknown language is used as an evidence that the fullness has arrived. Satan is always present to bring unbelief and doubt as to the genuineness of the things of God. He may endeavor to cause a person to doubt as to who or what is the cause of these feelings and this phenomenon. He may suggest that it was only the flesh, such as nervousness, a chill, self-hypnotism, or that it was some psychological phenomenon, such as thought-transference or some hypnotic influence exerted by others. He may even go so far as to suggest that it was a demon. In all this he might be successful if it were not for this last manifestation of speaking in the unknown language. When a person feels himself in the hands of a supernatural power that uses his vocal organs to speak in some language unknown to himself, he knows that it is not his own mind that is doing it. He may doubt as to whether it is the power of God or not. But when he finds that these utterances consist of praises and worship to Jesus and adoration of God, and bring the very presence of heaven into his soul, he knows that it must be God. For Satan never yet has magnified Jesus, and never will. This banishes all doubt and leaves the person assured and certain that the whole performance has been of the Lord.

When that complete yieldance has taken place which enables the Spirit to take such full possession as to speak thru that person at His own wish and will, it brings a feeling of intense satisfaction and the supply-

THE INFILLING AND ITS EVIDENCE

ing of that longing and soul-hunger for God and the things of God that may have existed for years.

Not Full Perfection — This does not mean that the full perfection immediately sets in, but rather that this arrival at fullness and presence of the Spirit enables the Spirit to more completely take charge of that life and lead on from truth to truth, and reveal the height, length, breadth and depth of the mysteries of godliness as never before. Rather than a finished experience, it becomes a more complete beginning.

CHAPTER XIV

The General Gifts of the Spirit

The Spirit Decides These manifestations of the Spirit, which so convinced the world of the genuineness and reality of the gospel, are administered by the Spirit thru His having imparted various gifts to those into whom He has come to take up His abode. The administration of these gifts is not dependent upon the wish and will of the person to whom they are imparted, but upon the Holy Spirit, for He "divideth unto each one severally even as He will." Consequently no one person's experience or enduement can become a standard or criterion for others. Each person is a case by himself, and its outcome is dependent upon no one but the Holy Spirit's own personal wish and desire.

Talents Determine It seems that in some cases the Spirit's distribution of gifts is determined in a measure by the make-up and inherited characteristics of the individual person. Usually He imparts such gifts as the person can most readily lend himself to. The natural orator is anointed to become a preacher, and the one with an analytical mind becomes a teacher. The one for whom it is more natural to have great faith receives the gift of healing, and such as have a combination of strong will-power, great faith, and a fiery nature become endued with power for the working of miracles or the casting out of demons. Others who are very susceptible to spiritual influences are endued with the gift of discernment of spirits.

The Holy Spirit is wisdom personified, and nothing He ever does takes place at random or is an accident. While most often His dealings and the imparting of gifts are adjusted to the person's apparent temperament and general make-up, such is not always the case. He at times sees things in a person that the individual and others are not aware of, things both good and bad, and operates accordingly. For instance, a person has those natural talents which would most readily lend themselves to evangelism or being a prophet, but at the same time also has other acquired or inherited tendencies which tend toward self-exaltation and ruinous conceit. In such a case it may happen that the Holy Spirit will impart only a minor gift, for the time being, or possibly permanently none at all. He reasons that the person is better off with only a minor gift or none at all than possessing one which he could not handle, or which thru the person's weakness would open the way for great temptation or possible fall.

Natures Change Thru the anointing of the Spirit it has happened that persons who are apparently naturally timid have become completely changed in nature and developed a boldness in the things of God that is truly astonishing. Men that as boys have been almost too timid in school to recite or partake in programs or games, have become veritable trumpets for God against the things of evil, fearing neither man nor devil. Others who have been forward, and naturally proud and haughty, have become humble and submissive. Just how and why these things are, is hard to say, but it has happened in hundreds of cases, always to the blessing and edification of the individual and to the good of God's cause. It seems that the baptism of the Holy Spirit rouses up every physiological force and power, both hidden and apparent, within a person. Sometimes these hidden and almost unknown characteristics have really been the better ones and of more value than those most commonly brought into play. These more desirable but almost submerged traits the Holy Spirit will bring forth and develop to the extent of dominating those less desirable. This of course will produce a change in nature, and in a measure explains that new order of things which comes into most lives at new birth and more often at receiving the baptism of the Spirit.

Humbleness Necessary Unless a person remains humble and walks close to the Lord, this rousing up of all these forces may produce a spirit of individualism which becomes very destructive to the person himself and makes it almost unbearable for those with whom he comes in contact. This spirit of individualism is primarily due to selfishness and conceit, and these two mixed with power make a very dangerous combination which often gives rise to the misuse of authority. It often happens that the person who has been filled with the Holy Spirit loses that spirit of humbleness which is so necessary in order to receive it, and becomes obsessed with the thought of his own importance. He feels a little better or bigger than others and soon shows it. The baptism of the Spirit is a wonderful gift and cannot be valued too highly; but it never ought to make a person boastful or cause him to act as tho he were too holy to speak to common people, or beyond receiving advice or admonition from others.

Some of the gifts of the Spirit, such as healing the sick, discernment of spirits, casting out of demons, and the anointing to preach and teach the Word, producing prophecy in its first forms, can be possessed in a measure before the full baptism occurs. While others, such as speaking with tongues and the interpretation thereof, the deeper phases of prophecy and discernment of spirits, the working of miracles and the casting out of the more powerful demons, cannot be possessed before the full baptism has taken place.

Fractional Gifts   Some may question why this is. As all true Christians have some measure of the Spirit, this measure manifests itself in some way, and the decree of this manifestation is directly determined by the degree in which the Holy Spirit has control over the individual. If the person has but partly yielded He has but a partial or fractional control over him, and therefore His operations are but partial or fractional; that is, there will be a mixture in the manifestation or operation, part Holy Spirit, and part the flesh and mind of the individual. Healings of the sick can take place under such conditions, also a small measure of discernment, likewise the casting out of the less powerful demons, and the ordinary preaching of the Word under a partial anointing. But the deeper and more powerful manifestations cannot take place because their successful operation is independent of the ordinary workings of the mind. In fact, in order to come forth in clearness and purity, the will and mind of the person, for that particular time and moment, must be so completely subject to and under the control of the Holy Spirit, that His wish and will are in no way interfered with. Unless in that condition of complete submissiveness to the Spirit of God the mind will interfere and effectually prevent the operation and manifestation of the Spirit. Thus it becomes evident that certain of these gifts and manifestations cannot take place unless the baptism has occurred, not because the experience has made the person any more worthy, but because the experience has prepared him in such a way that the Spirit can more successfully operate thru him and upon him.

The Human Will In some of the gifts the Holy Spirit can operate by using the will of the person. He suggests His will and the will of the person agrees therewith. But in others He operates independent of the person's will, not against it by any means, but rather in that He for the time being clothes Himself with that person's body and uses its faculties and powers as an instrument in His hand. These are peculiar things and hard to understand unless experienced, but once tasted of will never be forgotten. But before He can successfully clothe Himself with a human body that person must be completely surrendered to Him.

Why Obtain More Others may question the particular value of pressing on beyond the condition ordinarily arrived at in receiving salvation. Why seek these deeper things? Among other things, this deeper experience of receiving the baptism of the

THE GENERAL GIFTS OF THE SPIRIT   143

Spirit is of great value to the individual himself. The Spirit of God not only works thru a person, but also in him. In doing so He brings forth the fruits of the Spirit, which when more fully developed produce the very image of Christ. He also operates in us, and develops and reveals that "Christ in you, the hope of glory," which Paul speaks of, the receiving of which constitutes salvation. If we are only partly yielded, His development of the fruits of the Spirit and revelation of Christ is only partial, and as a result the person lacks many things he should have. But with that fuller yieldedness which is so necessary in order to receive the baptism, the Holy Spirit is less hindered and more free to bring these things forth. So the more of the Spirit a man has, the more he can get out of salvation.

But He also works thru us. We know that the Holy Spirit must have instruments to work with and channels to flow thru. In most cases His operations and accomplishments are directly determined by the capacity of the instrument or channel. An electric power plant of thousands of horsepower capacity cannot deliver any more power to a distant city than the connecting power line can safely transmit. The remainder goes unused. Neither can a power plant deliver any more energy toward moving an electric train than the motors of the locomotive can stand without injury. If they are heavy and powerful enough the train moves. If not, the train is unmoved, altho the power plant may have enough capacity to move a train ten times that size.

Limiting Factors   Many times God has a work to do and more than power enough to do it, but has to leave the work undone because He cannot find a channel or an instrument of sufficient capacity to operate thru. The man at His disposal is a good man and has considerable anointing, but that measure of the Spirit which can operate thru him is not sufficient to overcome the resistance produced by the condition met. The job, in other words, is too big for the man. Now if he were more yielded, the Spirit could in a greater measure operate thru him, and the greater degree in which he was yielded would allow a great enough measure of the Spirit to flow thru him to accomplish the work to be done. And the greater measure in which he yielded the more the Spirit could operate thru him and accomplish. If the yielding were absolute and complete the Spirit's operation would be unlimited and the things brought about infinite. This condition was present in Jesus, so that thru Him the Holy Spirit could work without measure. Many a person who is doing much now could do much more if he had a greater anointing. And the baptism of the Spirit would supply this, not only thru the gifts themselves, but thru the fact that the degree of yieldedness which enables the gifts to come forth would put him in a position where the Holy Spirit would have him more completely at His disposal.

For Edification The thought may arise as to the definite value of the gifts and their resulting manifestations. Paul says, in the epistle to the Ephesians, that they are "for the perfecting of the saints, unto the work of ministering, unto the building up of the body of Christ—that we may be no longer children, tossed to and fro." Evidently then they have a purpose and God had an object in view in bestowing

THE GENERAL GIFTS OF THE SPIRIT 145

them. So the question arises as to whether we can profitably live in Christ and successfully do the work of the Lord without them. The text seems to show that these operations of the Spirit are of peculiar advantage to the individual member, and also to the body of Christ. By blessing and developing each member the effectiveness and structure of the church, as a whole, are built up. Surely the church to-day needs the operation of the Holy Spirit and the true operation of His gifts, in order that the individual members of it may stand in this evil day, and that she may possess the heavenly dynamite which will enable her to overcome the present deepening and darkening clouds of demonic pressure and activity.

CHAPTER XV

Prophecy

Prophecy Because prophecy not only brought a bless-
Greatest ing to the prophet but unto all that heard,
Gift and thereby produced a collective blessing,
Paul rates it as the greatest and most valuable gift of all. On the day of Pentecost the one hundred and twenty spoke in tongues and caused the people to wonder and be puzzled. It brought such a blessing to those speaking that they staggered like drunken men, but no converts were produced until Peter, filled with the Holy Spirit, spoke a language which they all understood and to which three thousand gave heed. The operation of the gift of healing upon the lame man at the temple gate blessed Peter and John, and most of all, the man himself, so that he leaped and praised God and caused the gathered multitude to wonder greatly. But beyond these three there were no results unto salvation until Peter boldly proclaimed unto them the resurrected Christ, as a result of which God's power gripped five thousand who had listened. In each case it seems as tho the operation of the minor gift paved the way and set the stage for the operation of the greater one.

Besides being of great blessing to the many,
Personal the gift of prophecy brings great blessings
Blessing to the person himself. So does the operation

of all the gifts, even that of the Spirit of intercession and travail in prayer which leaves a person too weak at times to even stand. So does the speaking in tongues and for this reason Paul wished that they all spoke with tongues, not because it was of any particular value to others, but because it brought blessing to the one speaking. Preaching, however, does not always bring blessing to the one speaking, as some preaching is nothing more or less than the physical and mental operation of the mind and body without any presence of the Holy Spirit whatever. But speaking under the anointing of the Spirit becomes prophecy. This anointing of the Spirit is something vastly different from any such thing as personal magnetism, personal or collective enthusiasm, or a fiery nature.

Like Unto Fire   This anointing has many ways of manifesting itself. At times it may come gradually as the speaker warms up to his subject. Or he may feel the presence of the Spirit come upon him long before the service commences and abide with him until needed. Sometimes when a service is hard and there is a resistance in the air, due either to the operation of demons or opposing minds in the audience, right in the midst of the message as he is laboring and struggling to get the truth out, this anointing may strike him like a bolt of lightning from heaven and pass thru his frame like a powerful electric shock and even affect the whole audience. Or it may happen that as he sits on the platform waiting for the time to speak, often without any particular message and wondering what he shall say, this anointing may come upon him like a mighty wave of electricity or molten liquid fire and passing thru his whole body make every muscle, nerve and fiber tingle and tremble under the influence of the Spirit of God, and at the same time bring the message needed for the time and place, and the necessary power to give it forth. These waves feel like a flame that burns into the very marrow of the bones and even produces a strong sensation of heat, but which instead of being painful like an electric current, is very beautiful and satisfying. It surely reminds the person of the promise, "He shall baptize you in the Holy Spirit and in fire." These manifestations leave a wonderful blessing that lasts as long as the man speaks and at times even for days afterwards. They take away all man-fear and timidity and make the person bold and fearless. They also drive away any tiredness in the flesh. The person's body may be tired almost to the point of exhaustion, but this fire seems to neutralize those poisonous fatigue-toxins in the muscles and the blood and drive out that sensation of fatigue and tiredness, even at times satisfying as much as a refreshing sleep.

Refreshing If due to demonic pressure the body is heavy and the mind feels as tho it were bound, dull, heavy and unresponsive, then the waves of fire will relieve it in a few moments. There is something peculiar about this. If there are several waves each wave will do a portion. The first relieves in a degree, the next still more, and so on until complete deliverance arrives. And they may also vary in intensity. At times they may come so mightily as to leave the person almost helpless for a few moments or even staggering as tho drunk. Or they may bring on a state of being in a trance and the person may have visions and revelations. It seems that this fire breaks down the resistance of the flesh and of the mind and opens the way for the Spirit to rest upon the person for a shorter or longer period.

If from excessive mental effort the mind is fatigued and too heavy to think clearly or form connected thoughts, this fire will bring a feeling as tho a curtain were being rolled back off the brain, and this curtain remains rolled back and the brain functions normally or even better, as long as the anointing rests. But as soon as the anointing leaves the tiredness returns with interest. When physical tiredness, due to muscular exercise, is removed, it does not return with the anointing's removal, but the body remains fresh until again made tired by exercise. But this is not the case with the mind. Its tiredness returns as soon as the anointing leaves and it is often left almost exhausted.

There seems to be some connection between the psychological forces within a person and the operations of the Holy Spirit thru him. Apparently this operation, at least in a measure, consists of making use of not understood and even hidden forces within a person, and in the course of the Spirit's operation these forces are used up and need to be replenished. It also appears that the degree of His operation thru the person is considerably dependent upon the quantity of this force and power at His disposal. This remarkable expression is found in the Hebrew text of the Old Testament, "The Holy Spirit clothed itself with Gideon" (and others.) This can mean nothing more or less than that the Holy Spirit actually used the man's body as a garment, and made use of all the man's faculties, both physical and mental, known and unknown, as instruments by which and thru which He accomplished His work. The Holy Spirit proceeding forth from the Father has no body of His own, and there are some things which it appears He cannot accomplish except one is at His disposal.

Virtue Flows Out   This operation of the anointing and drawing upon the mental and psychological forces under the influence of the Spirit, brings a feeling upon the person as tho something were flowing out of him. This may be what Jesus felt when He said that virtue had flowed out of Him when the woman touched the hem of His garment. The larger the audience and the more powerful the anointing, the more this is felt. The flowing out of this virtue leaves a person very tired. The audience feels that it is receiving something. Something has gone from the speaker to them. It is this outflow of virtue that makes a preacher interesting, and makes all the difference between an interesting and an uninteresting sermon. There are men who do not know what this means and have never felt it. These as a rule, altho very intelligent and deep thinkers, never are interesting speakers. Their message sounds better read than spoken.

This outflow of virtue is very tiring and rest is needed. It seems that the mind is more slow at recovering from exhaustion than the body, so that more sleep and food are needed than when engaged in physical labor. This outflow of virtue also takes place when being used for the healing of the sick. Sometimes praying for a number of persons will leave the one so doing very tired. But still more so this is felt in the casting out of demons. If the demons are powerful and resist, the result of the battle may leave the person who casts them out unable to even stand, and often requiring immediate food and sleep. The person exercised by the Spirit of God needs to take a rest, lest he allow more virtue to flow out in the course of protracted services or exercise of the gift, than sleep or food can normally supply. Times of withdrawal are often needed and will be found very beneficial.

In the course of revival work or extended meetings this anointing may rest upon the speaker continuously, causing a feeling of ecstacy to remain upon him at all times. Then he can preach at a moment's notice and conviction sets in upon the audience immediately.

Anointing Evidences Call — To bring this anointing the man himself must be fully yielded to God. Some feel this in a measure before they receive the baptism, but in each instance after receiving the baptism it comes with tenfold increased power. Apparently the degree of yieldance necessary to bring about the baptism puts the man in position where the Holy Spirit can rest more heavily upon him and more completely use him. There are those who never feel any of the anointing before receiving the baptism, and even afterward experience but little of it. Why this is, it is hard to say. But one thing is certain. Every man truly called of God is prepared for that calling by receiving some measure of the anointing of the Spirit. It may well be added that if a man is attempting to preach without any measure of the presence of the power of the Spirit, and never has tasted of it, we have a right before God to question his call and ministry and wonder if he could not more profitably put in his time at something else.

The anointing also brings physical blessing. A man may be sick in body, with a heavy cold, a toothache or rheumatism, or tormented with a splitting headache, but on the arrival of the fire from heaven be instantly relieved, to last as long as the anointing lasts or possibly may be permanently healed.

The measure of the anointing resting upon the speaker is in a considerable degree dependent upon the spiritual condition of the place and the assembly. If the spiritual condition of the people is good and there is no resistance due to opposing minds or divisions in the assembly, the anointing can come very powerfully. The presence of unsaved who are open for conviction will almost invariably bring great liberty if the man is in any way responsive. Considerable prayer by the people for the speaker will usually bring the anointing, even tho he has not done much praying himself, but it is not anywhere nearly as effective as when he also has prayed. A man who takes time to wait upon God almost invariably preaches under the influence of the Spirit. If some men spent less time hunting up other people's opinions and digging thru the products of other minds and spent more time on their knees, there would be more fire in the pulpit.

But the anointing can also come when there is demonic or mental resistance resting upon a gathering, and it is under these conditions that the most powerful manifestations of the Spirit come forth. It often happens that in conventions and allied gatherings, Satan attempts to spoil the plan and wish of God by using unconsecrated minds to inject irrelevant thoughts and ideas, and thereby sidetrack the whole purpose and trend of things into some practically valueless side issues. If, then, prayer and supplication is made by several, or by only one who knows the will of God for that particular place and gathering, the Holy Spirit's power can and often has come upon someone so mightily as to give a message that will completely overthrow all opposition and swing the whole gathering into line.

Some are very sensitive to the workings of the Spirit, and can tell the outcome of a convention or campaign by the degree of His presence or absence days in advance. Often as much as a week before, the Spirit will come upon the person again and again, covering a period of several days, both during the day and at night, preparing the person, as it were, for the work to come. In a consecrated pastor's work and ministry he will often notice waves of the presence and absence of the Spirit. For periods covering as much as several months, or more, he will feel a dryness and dearth upon himself and his people, with a more or less lack of liberty in giving forth the Word. Then again will come times of refreshing, when it is easy to preach, added interest prevails and souls are being saved. What may be the exact cause of this is hard to say, but it is probably due to the surgings back and forth in the battle between the power of God and the unseen demonic principalities and powers in the heavenly places.

Easily Quenched   It requires holy living, prayer and a close walk with God to keep this anointing, and it does not take many foolish words or fleshly actions to lose it. Sin in a life will drive it away almost instantly, and it will remain away unless the sin is repented of or righted. Many men who once possessed this blessing are to-day without it for this very reason.

It is this presence and operation of the Spirit which makes the difference between plain preaching and a message from God, between a man operating in his own strength and one laboring in the strength of the Lord, and between the man giving forth his own ideas and one preaching the Word. Under the anointing any message on salvation is interesting irrespective of whether the grammar and pronunciation are correct or the language perfect. But without it the most carefully thought out and perfect sermon may be as dry as a bone.

Various Forms In some men's ministry, for instance, the Holy Spirit's operation may be limited to some one method peculiar to that man himself. The others he may know nothing about. With another it may be a diversity of ways, with one or two more prominent and common. With still another there may be practically no limit, each time, place and condition receiving its own necessary manifestation in the measure and degree that it is there needed. Therefore it is impossible to lay down any hard and fast rules governing the operation of this gift of prophecy. Each one thankfully accepts what he receives, all the while asking God for more in order that his ministry may become effective.

Lesser In its milder and most common form, especially present among those who have not received the baptism and in a measure found among those who have, the Holy Spirit will prepare the man for his message while he is studying. The mind so blessed will become exceptionally keen to grasp the truth being read. A clear insight into the subject on hand will be given and with it the ability to arrange the facts so as to become most effective upon presentation. A man so prepared by the Spirit will feel certain of his text and subject, and an assurance of its successful delivery. On delivering such a message he will feel that he has his subject well in hand and that little or no irrelevant matter enters in. He will often find that his mind is very clear and functioning perfectly. It usually happens that under these conditions he will feel a gentle and sweet presence of the Spirit upon himself and his audience, altho this presence at times may become quite pronounced.

Greater A less common but more powerful and effective operation is when the Spirit Himself gives the topic or text. This He may do several hours or only a few minutes before speaking. Sometimes it does not arrive until the man enters the pulpit. When the text or topic is thus given it is usually accompanied by a flash of the power of the Spirit, with a feeling like fire thru the flesh of the one who is to speak. This flash of power instantly clears the mind of the speaker takes away any physical or mental fatigue, and removes any man-fearing spirit, making him bold and fearless. Its effect upon the audience will be to anoint the ears and minds of the people to hear and understand; any heavy, depressing atmosphere will leave, and the gathering become quiet even to the little children. Such as find themselves prone to doze discover themselves strangely awake. The speaker often feels a tingling in his flesh, and a sensation akin to fire resting upon him. If this becomes powerful it may even be felt by those in the audience. His mind becomes as clear as crystal, and the thoughts flow as freely as water, with a consciousness of great freedom and liberty in the Spirit. The mind seems to operate supernormally, and thoughts and ideas never before experienced come one after another. Questions puzzled at and reasoned over while in study, suddenly unravel with astonishing clearness. Information and facts, read years before and long forgotten, readily and accurately present themselves. Intricate questions, hard to understand, are easily grasped and presented in such a way that the simplest can understand. Often the audience feels as tho it were under a spell, and a queer feeling permeates the atmosphere. If the message is on salvation, a powerful conviction sets in and strong men find themselves shaking, while others are moved to tears. At times, under these conditions, the Spirit will bring forth some strange things. After one such service in which a certain woman was saved, she remarked, "You told me my whole life history. I first thought that someone had told you all about me and that you were taking public occasion to speak directly to me, and to me alone." Another remarked, "The first time I heard you preach I was certain that someone who knew that I was coming, had told you all about me, and that you were publicly ridiculing me. I went home angry, resolved never to to come back again. But being puzzled over what had happened the first time, I returned to see if it would happen again. Again I felt the thoughts of my heart literally laid open, and again I angrily resolved never to come back. But, nevertheless, I returned the third time, and then realizing that only God could speak directly to a person and bring forth things of this nature thru another ignorant of them, I surrendered to Him."

Value of Education In this type of anointing the Holy Spirit uses the mind of the person, and naturally the better equipped and more developed that mind is, the better He can use it and the more He can accomplish. The Holy Spirit's operations are practically always limited to the caliber of the instrument He uses. A well read mind, well stocked with facts systematically arranged and covering a great range of subjects, becomes an excellent tool in His hand. Then the Spirit has a large storehouse at His disposal and arranging the material to suit the subject He can present a masterpiece of logic and reasoning. When used in the pulpit independent of the power of the Spirit, education alone is often of very little value and sometimes dangerous. But coupled with the power of God, it becomes very effective. Education, self-acquired or school learned, gives a man an accumulation of knowledge. During the process of receiving it the mind has become sharpened, it has learned to think and has developed. This sharpened mind, with its accumulation of knowledge, becomes a far more ready and effective tool in the hands of the Spirit than one not so sharpened and without any accumulation of knowledge. By all means let us educate, but let us be careful how we do it, and, most of all, see that education is not considered of more value than the Holy Spirit, and that it is not used as a substitute for the power of God.

Under this type of anointing the Spirit directs the activities of the mind, and reveals to it and thru it the contents of the Scriptures. This knowledge may disagree with the person's own previous opinion on the subject, but, needless to say, is always orthodox. Such knowledge once imparted is never forgotten, and when later brought forth is always honored by the Spirit's presence and power. Many a preacher's theology today consists of, and has been built up from, what the Spirit has imparted directly to his mind while in the pulpit. Such men are not prone to chase heresies, nor are they easily swept off their feet by these modern attempts at modernizing the gospel. If a man early in his ministry could be sufficiently yielded to receive this direct revelation by the Spirit, of the contents of the Word, he would never need to change his theology, nor regret in the future years what he may have preached in the past. He would feel that what he has is from God and for which there would be no need of apology.

It may also happen that the anointing may not arrive until after the man has been speaking for some time. Terrific resistance of various kinds and origins may have hindered the Spirit from coming forth and resting upon the speaker or the gathering. But as the service goes on the resistance becomes gradually or suddenly broken. If gradually, then the subject may gradually change and the service which started, dry, lifeless and listless, will develop into one of interest. Or the Spirit may strike like a flash of fire and instantly clearing the atmosphere change the whole spirit and course of the service, stopping the message being delivered and giving a new text on a new subject. Such happenings are not common, and it takes a man well yielded and with a strong sense of discernment to be used in this way.

Greatest Form The most powerful form of the anointing and operation of the gift of prophecy, and therefore the most effective, is quite rare and vastly different from any of the others. In the former types, the Spirit has used the mind by suggesting thoughts and ideas, but in the latter it seems that the mind itself is sidetracked and the Holy Spirit personally assumes complete control of the whole being and of every faculty in it. The Spirit literally clothes Himself with the person as a garment and uses his faculties as instruments. In the former types, the mind has operated under the control and influence of the Spirit, but in this latter one the mind actually seems to cease to function. Instead of being the source of the thoughts it becomes a listener, and the person speaking hears and enjoys what is being said as much as anyone in the audience. The person feels as tho some mighty supernatural power takes possession of his body, and that he himself becomes a spectator to the operations that follow. This power does not seem to send out its flow of energy from the mind, but rather from the inward parts of the abdomen. Possibly this is what Jesus had in mind when He said, "From within him shall flow rivers of living water." And John explains, "This spake he of the Spirit, which they that believed on him were to receive: for the Spirit was not yet given." And surely it does feel as tho rivers of something were flowing out. There also comes a sensation of fullness to the point of bursting, as tho one were filled with some terrific pent-up force desiring outlet. Unless given vent to, this may increase so as to make breathing labored and bring a powerful trembling upon the body, and the presence of the Spirit so strong as to be unable to sit or stand. But if the person yields, this power takes control of the vocal organs, the throat, lips and tongue of the person, and speaks the language common to the people or gathering, bringing forth the deep things of God, and often using the personal pronoun "I."

All the operations of the gift of prophecy bring blessing upon the audience, but this form of it brings greater blessing than any of the others; and produces the greatest results. It is never known to have occurred to one who has not received the full baptism, and it is quite rare among those who have. Greater yieldance is needed for this than for receiving the baptism itself. Almost invariably, it is accompanied by a deluge of the power of God upon the gathering, often with pronounced results for salvation and repentance. One Sunday morning a pastor had thought of speaking along a certain line, and had prepared accordingly. As the service commenced the atmosphere seemed as usual, but as he stepped up to speak and opened his Bible to read, a peculiar something came upon him and also upon the people, arresting his attention. This increased, and an intense stillness and feeling of awe came over all. Several were moved to tears. Suddenly he felt a powerful shock go thru his whole body, followed by another, and another, until he seemed lost in God. The power of the Spirit rested mightily upon him, and he felt the Spirit take hold of and control his lips and tongue, and speak thru him in English for some three or four minutes at a time, with intermission, covering in all a period of some fifteen minutes. By the end of that time almost every one in the place was weeping, some calling out for salvation, and others for the return of their first love. Many that had for a long time resisted the effects of the Word and the conviction of the Spirit, found themselves unable to hold out any longer, and surrendered. This condition lasted for several hours, and more or less continued all day.

Sometimes it may happen that while a person is speaking under a lesser anointing, this more powerful manifestation suddenly comes on, lasting for a few minutes, and this may be in the form of a prophetic message foretelling things to come to pass. Once a pastor, who for some years had served in a place, was there closing his ministry. In the last message, as he stood before the people the presence of the Spirit was very pronounced upon the gathering. In the midst of his talk he felt this added measure of the Spirit, and to his own surprise began to tell what the church would go thru in the future and its ultimate results for the coming years. All were melted to tears, and time proved the statements absolutely correct.

It was very probably this form of the gift of prophecy which operated in the apostles and prophets of old. Old Zacharias, the father of John the Baptist, felt this when he prophesied at John's birth; likewise Mary, the mother of Jesus, on coming into Elizabeth's house. The old prophets knew what it was to feel the power of God to the point of bursting, for Jeremiah complains about forbearing until unable to do so any longer. Isaiah's utterances were not the product of his own mind, but were the clear, well-worded statements of the Holy Spirit speaking thru him. Some of the things he said he hardly understood himself. Oh, let us pray that God may raise up more men that He can speak thru! The world is perishing and the Word of God is rarely heard. Men are substituting their own utterances for "Thus saith Jehovah."

CHAPTER XVI

Speaking With Tongues

Compared With Prophecy Like true prophecy, speaking in tongues can only occur after the full baptism of the Holy Spirit has taken place. As far as the Spirit's operation and feelings upon the person are concerned these manifestations are alike, but they differ in results, in that the one gives forth a language that is understood and the other is an unknown tongue. As in the most powerful forms of prophecy, this operation seems to proceed forth from one's inward parts. The mind is temporarily a spectator, with the ears listening to what is being said. The sensations are as tho some living thing "in the inward parts," as the Scripture puts it, for the time being takes control of the vocal organs, speaking mysteries.

This manifestation comes forth in several different forms and it is the inability to differentiate between these, both as to their value and government, that has caused so much confusion and misuse on the part of those who possess it, and opposition from those who do not. These forms are divided into two parts: those manifestations which come forth in the public meeting, such as the message in the tongue which always ought to be interpreted, and those which ought to be limited to private worship. It might be well to remember that Paul's advice to the Corinthians as to use and misuse of the speaking in the unknown tongue is concerning its operations in the assembly. About its manifestation in the private worship he says but little.

Three Forms   In private worship this manifestation becomes of greatest value as far as the individual is concerned. At such times the unknown tongue becomes the utterances of the indwelling Spirit speaking directly to God, and this occurs in three more common forms, prayer in the Spirit, worship and praise in the Spirit, and singing in the Spirit. All of these are very beautiful and edifying to the individual and bring a condition of intense spiritual ecstasy.

Prayer in Spirit   In prayer in the Spirit, the Holy Spirit Himself does the praying, but, as Paul puts it, the "understanding is unfruitful." 1 Cor. 14:14. This prayer and petition may be for the person himself or may be for others. It may be for things and conditions of which he has knowledge, or it may be for things of which he is in total ignorance. Paul speaks of praying with the Spirit and praying with the understanding. In praying with the understanding our mind is operative, and our prayers and petitions are according to its desires and knowledge of conditions and persons. Prayer with the understanding is good, but it has its limitations. If the capacity of our minds were infinite and consequently our knowledge likewise, there would be no bounds to what prayer with the understanding could accomplish. But as it is, our capacity for prayer in this form is to the largest extent limited to our knowledge of conditions and persons, and this most often at its best is very meager. There are conditions and things of which the human mind has no knowledge except as supernaturally revealed by the Spirit of God; such as demon activities, or events about to transpire. Against such, prayer with the understanding can make no preparation and affords but little protection. But God, knowing our limited knowledge and abilities along this line, has made provision by providing prayer in the Spirit which supplies what prayer with the understanding lacks. This the Holy Spirit is well capable of doing, for He has all knowledge, is everywhere present, and searches the deep things of God. Thru this searching He knows God's plan concerning any person or assembly and by making petition beforehand makes preparation for its fulfillment. Thru His being everywhere present and possessing all knowledge, He knows just what plans for evil are being laid by the powers of darkness, and using a human body as an instrument can make supplication to the throne of grace that these plans be frustrated. Such power is far beyond the possibilities of any human mind or understanding.

In this praying in the Spirit the one so doing may know what is being prayed for, or he may not. He may know in a general way that it is for a certain person, or place, or condition, but not know what is being asked.

Some years ago a certain missionary was leaving for China. Several persons were strangely and powerfully exercised in prayer in the Spirit for this young woman, but none knew just why, except that they felt that grave danger lay ahead. As nothing developed immediately they wondered at the authenticity and genuineness of their manifestation. After a time conditions became manifest at the place she was staying, and in the surrounding country also, that boded great danger to herself physically and spiritually. Then the reason for this prayer in the Spirit almost two years in advance became evident.

In another instance a minister of the gospel far from home, thru the devil operating in selfish Christians, was put in a very difficult position that tested his salvation to the extreme, and left him exceedingly puzzled as to know what to do. Unable to move one way or the other, he felt strangely admonished in the Spirit just to remain quiet and watch the Lord handle the whole situation. The Lord wonderfully undertook and poured out His Spirit marvelously to the dumbfounding and confounding of all opposition. In a few days he received a letter from Minnesota stating that, at a certain time, a friend felt admonished to pray for him in the Spirit. And this agreed with the time that he was so sorely tried. Some weeks later a letter from China stated that a person there had been likewise exercised, and the time again coincided.

At another time a servant of the Lord, arriving at a friend's home, found himself ill but unable to tell what was the matter. During the night this illness increased to a high fever, congestion of the lungs, with an aching over the whole body. Sleep came fitfully or not at all. Some hours after midnight his attention was attracted by hearing someone praying in the Spirit in another room. This prayer became more and more intense, but after some ten or fifteen minutes changed to a song of praise, following which it ceased. Much relieved in mind and body, and confident that the Holy Spirit Himself had made petition, he fell asleep. In the morning he was still sick and much too weak to arise.

While lying there somewhat puzzled over the happenings in the night and debating on what this might lead to, he felt several strong shocks of the power of God pass thru his body, bringing great relief, but not enough to be able to arise. A few minutes later several more came, much more violent and powerful than the first, and lasting longer. These left him completely well and he arose immediately. Soon one of the household said, "Last night I was suddenly awakened and told to pray for you. I was puzzled to know why, but obeyed orders, and immediately the Holy Spirit began making supplication. At first it seemed very hard, but after a while the victory came and with it a song of praise, by which I knew that everything would be all right. No longer burdened I fell asleep." The Holy Spirit, knowing what was going on, had awakened another who was ignorant of what was amiss, to make the necessary petition.

A saintly mother had a son at sea. One night she was awakened and strongly impressed to pray, feeling that a ship, name unknown, was in danger of being wrecked on Peacock Spit, a dangerous point near the mouth of the Columbia River, a place much dreaded by all navigators. The next morning her son unexpectedly arrived home, and she related her experience. Then he told her that during the night, as the ship was proceeding toward Portland, his vessel thru the combined influence of the strong wind and tide, narrowly escaped being wrecked at this point.

A young woman to all intents was dying. The life process had gradually become less and less, and the senses of seeing and hearing and consciousness had ebbed out in the order named. One at each side of the bed was feeling the pulse, and the breath became more and more labored, further and further apart, and at last apparently ceased altogether. At the same time the heart beats, which had been becoming weaker and weaker, with pauses between, could no longer be felt, and as far as could be detected had stopped. The two attendants and the husband had been praying for hours, but to no avail. Suddenly the power of the Spirit struck the husband, and in a loud and powerful voice and in an unknown tongue he prayed for at least a minute. The pulse fluttered feebly at first, and slowly commenced beating, and with it came a gasp of breath. Both breathing and heart action became stronger and stronger, and consciousness and the senses returned in the reversed order in which they had left. The next noon the young woman was sitting in a chair dressed, weak, but to all intents normal.

This prayer in the Spirit very often resolves itself into a petition for some soul's salvation, but usually does not take place until the person is under very heavy conviction and is deliberately resisting, or is bound by some demon. The Spirit seldom prays more than once in this way for a person. If they resist this they are usually left to their fate and the grieved Spirit, having done His uttermost, withdraws, and those trying to pray for the person find it practically impossible and useless to do so.

For prayer in the Spirit to bring the best results the person must be even more yielded to God than is necessary to receive the baptism. For this reason many of those who possess the baptism have never experienced it and know absolutely nothing about it. For the Spirit to obtain the petition asked He must pray, and this He cannot do unless He has full control. Many, not knowing how to yield, allow so much of their own flesh to come in that the Holy Spirit cannot accomplish the desired results.

Praise   In private worship the unknown tongue may
in   come forth in the form of praise, the Holy
Spirit   Spirit offering praises to God. This manifestation is very beautiful and exceedingly edifying to the individual. It quite often occurs after a season of prayer in the Spirit, and is an evidence that the petition is granted and that the Spirit has prayed thru. But it may also resolve itself into a worship of God, the Spirit speaking mysteries unto the Lord. As this praising the Lord in the unknown tongue increases in intensity, the person may enter into a state of prophetic ecstasy and even trance, and see visions or prophecy. Needless to say, this experience goes beyond the ability of words to describe and must be tasted to be understood. These are holy moments when the person's own spirit deals directly with his Maker, and things unutterable are often revealed. During times of deep worship in the Spirit the person feels literally moved out of the present world and presented to the very door of heaven, and in the Spirit sees what the eye has not seen, and hears what the ear has not heard, and has revealed those things that never have entered into the heart of man, whatsoever things God has prepared for them that love Him.

Singing   This worship in the Spirit may have com-
in   menced as prayer in the understanding, and
Spirit   as the power of God increased it became utterances in the unknown tongue. These ut-

terances may be just isolated words, such as expressions of endearment and love, or may be whole sentences and paragraphs of praise and thanksgiving. At times they may come in poetical meter and rhythm, and when such are usually in the form of songs of praise. This is what Paul calls singing in the Spirit. The most beautiful melodies may come forth. The voice seems to become supernatural in tone and range, and the Holy Spirit may so manipulate the vocal organs as to sound as tho two persons were singing. The best opera singing is flat in comparison. This is exceedingly soul-ravishing to those who may be listening, and brings an atmosphere and presence of heaven that is indescribable and never forgotten. The one so exercised may be so lost in God as to hardly realize that he is singing. Very often the one singing is in a state of trance and hears music like great angelic choruses accompanied by heaven's orchestras, at one moment swelling and filling all creation, and then decreasing in volume until but one voice is heard, sweet as the glory of God itself. This may last for some minutes or for several hours. A person may be awakened in the still hours of the night and receive an experience like this, and then lay awake until morning and arise as refreshed as tho the whole night had been spent in sleep.

These manifestations of the unknown tongue, the intercessory prayer, the praise and worship, and the singing in the Spirit, are very probably the most edifying that the human body can experience, and when most intense, approach very close to the limit of what flesh and blood can stand and still remain in the land of the living.

SPEAKING WITH TONGUES

Intensely   They also bring a nearness of God that
Edifying   makes the person of God, heaven, and all
things spiritual very real. The earth and all that it contains seems to fade away, and heaven draws near. It seems as tho a veil were lifted, or a person were waking out of a sleep and entering into a new and very wonderful and different plane of existence. In this plane he feels very much at home and desires to remain, loathing to go back to the humdrum existence of the world's everyday activities. Possibly this is what the translation will be like and what we shall feel while our last breath is being taken and we sweetly slip into eternity and are taken away by the angels to be in the presence of Jesus.

Someone may ask what the attitude of the Scriptures is on this subject. Paul says, "I will pray with the spirit, and I will pray with the understanding also: I will sing with the spirit, and I will sing with the understanding also." 1 Cor. 14:15. Notice that he does not say "I will NOT pray or sing with the Spirit," but rather, "I will."

Of   By this it becomes evident that he will use both
Value   ways. But the question arises if this is not
contradictory to his own statement, "In the church I had rather speak five words with the understanding, that I might instruct others also, than ten thousand words in a tongue." No, they are not contradictory. If Paul had in mind to pray and sing in the Spirit in public they would be, but he had not. In public he desired to use such words and language as all understood and would be edified by. For this purpose five words understood by the audience are more effec-

tive than ten thousand words that are not. But when by himself and worshiping for his own edification he will use both ways of praying and singing in order to obtain the blessings that both bring, and these blessings he wanted, for he said, "I will pray—I will sing with the Spirit." Paul places no restrictions whatever on the use of the tongue when used in the right place. He values the tongue because of its edification, for he says, "I thank God, I speak with tongues more than you all." And he also says, "I would have you all speak with tongues." 1 Cor. 14:5. Surely he does not thank God for something that has no value, or wish that others might have a valueless manifestation. It is a great mistake to take what Paul says about governing the use of the tongue in the assembly and apply this to its use at all times and in all places.

Interpreted Message Another form of this manifestation is the message in the unknown tongue with the interpretation. This may occur in private worship, in a small prayer gathering, or in the general meeting. When the unknown tongue is interpreted in private worship it usually is a message direct to and concerning the person himself. If it occurs in a small prayer gathering it may be given by one and interpreted by another, and then usually is a message to someone present or the gathering as a whole. When the message in the unknown tongue comes forth in the general meeting it always should be interpreted. If no interpretation is given the one speaking should remain silent. "If any man speaketh in a tongue, let it be by two or at the most three, and that in turn; and let one interpret: but if there be no interpreter, let him keep silence in the church." 1 Cor. 14:27-28.

Paul seems to value this form of message quite highly. The prophetic message is of greater value than the one in the tongue, except the latter be interpreted, in which case it appears that both are equal. He says, "Greater is he that prophesieth than he that speaketh with tongues, except he interpret, that the church may receive edifying." The uninterpreted message is valueless as far as the church is concerned because the church receives no edification from it. But when it is interpreted it is not valueless, because the church then is blessed. In the direct prophetic message the Holy Spirit thru the person speaks direct to the people in a language that all can understand. In the interpreted message the Spirit first speaks a message that none can understand, and then thru the same person or thru another speaks the same thing in a language that all know. In the one case He speaks once, and in the other twice, to bring forth what He has to say. This interpreted message is just as distinct as pure prophecy and quite often more so, and when devoid of all flesh and interference of the mind is very edifying and upbuilding to those who may hear it.

This manifestation comes forth in a variety of ways, with hardly two persons affected alike or any two occurrences the same. No one person or occasion can be laid down as a standard or criterion.

During Quite often it comes as an interlude or in-
Sermon sertion into the message being preached. If
it is the speaker himself who speaks with the tongue he also usually gives the interpretation, or if

another sitting by or one in the audience speaks with the tongue, the preacher may also give the interpretation. Usually the one preaching can feel in the Spirit that such a message is coming and will pause for a moment to allow it to come forth. If he does not pause the power of God may come on the one exercised so mightily that he is unable to keep still, causing him to rise up and give it out even while the other is preaching. If the speaker is wise he will stop and allow the message to come forth and then wait for the interpretation to be given. The one who gives the message may interpret his own message or another may do so. When the Holy Spirit can work unhindered, the message in the tongue and its interpretation which comes forth in the midst of a sermon, becomes, and is, a part of the sermon being preached. It seems that when the Holy Spirit has something to say He can use two or three, or even more, human bodies to speak thru provided they are completely yielded to Him.

The Scriptural order seems to be that not too many messages shall come together. "If any man speaketh in a tongue, let it be by two, or at the most three."

Clears Atmosphere A message of this kind may come in the midst of a tight and trying service and be effective towards driving away the power of the enemy. A young woman, called of God to preach and much blessed in her ministry, in attempting to speak found the service and atmosphere very hard and oppressive. She stopped and said that it was of no use for her to continue any longer. After a few moments the power of the Spirit came mightily upon her and she gave a message in the unknown tongue and interpreted it. Instantly the air was cleared and great liberty came upon the meeting.

Or in a revival service it may come as a forerunner or bringer of a deluge of the presence of God, and pave the way for an effective working of the Holy Spirit covering a longer period. At one place a campaign had continued for some time without any apparent effect or results. As a result of special prayer services definitely asking for an outpouring of the power of God, the tide gradually commenced to rise. One Sunday morning as the preacher was about to preach the power of the Spirit came mightily upon him and others. Several messages were given in the tongue and interpreted, resulting in the salvation of many present. This outpouring then lasted several months to the salvation of many souls and the great blessing of all concerned. At another place several weeks of hard, protracted effort had brought nothing, and the power of the devil seemed to become stronger day by day. The saints were almost in despair but continued praying. One evening unexpectedly, the power of the Spirit came with a series of powerful utterances in the unknown tongue, which, interpreted, were rebukes against the power of Satan. Instantly the enemy fled, and for six weeks the power of God worked to the salvation of many.

During a revival terrific opposition was encountered due to a long-standing split in the assembly. Three weeks of prayer and intercession brought no results beyond added liberty in preaching. One evening the service commenced as usual with no liberty in singing or testimony. The power of the Spirit came upon a young married woman who for some minutes seemed lost in the ecstasy of quietly praising God. In a few minutes, a man thirty-five years of age, rose to his feet and gave several powerful messages in the tongue, all of which were interpreted by the man in the pulpit. From the time of the first message the power of God came upon the whole assembly and, increasing towards the last, it became so mighty that for a few minutes it felt as tho the coming of the Lord were at hand. Several became frightened and ran out. Others tried to crowd forward but fell headlong in the aisles. Still others fell out of the chairs, while others sat still, unable to move. After the first intense wave passed over an exceedingly powerful spirit of conviction settled down, and scores went to their knees praying for salvation. Backsliders who for some time had been unwilling to acknowledge their condition, did so and were reclaimed. Others who ran out came back in and were saved. It all came about in less than ten minutes and lasted for several hours.

Sometimes the interpreted message may come at the close of an evangelistic sermon and become a direct appeal to the unsaved to yield. This is very effective, and at times it feels as tho God Himself were speaking direct to the sinner.

It is recorded that on the day of Pentecost "they were all filled with the Holy Spirit, and began to speak with other tongues, as the Spirit gave them utterance." Acts 2:4. At Cornelius' household, "while Peter yet spake these words, the Holy Spirit fell on all them that heard the word. And they of the circumcision that believed were amazed, as many as came with Peter, because that on the Gentiles also was poured out the gift of the Holy Spirit. For they heard them speak with tongues, and magnify God." Acts 10:44-46. At

Ephesus Paul met some of John the Baptist's disciples. "And when Paul had laid his hands upon them, the Holy Spirit came on them; and they spake with tongues, and prophesied." Acts 19:6.

Baptism Most Bible students agree that the speak-
Evidence ing with the tongue as recorded in these
instances is not the same as the gift of tongues spoken of by Paul in Corinthians. Apparently the gift of tongues and the speaking with tongues as the Spirit gives utterance are not the same phenomenon. At Cesarea they of the circumcision were amazed when they saw that the Gentiles also had received the gift of the Holy Spirit, and the fact that the Spirit had been given became evident because "they heard them speak with tongues, and magnify God." The speaking with the other tongue became the evidence that the Holy Spirit had come upon them. These Jews knew what had happened to themselves when they had received the Holy Spirit, and when they saw the same thing taking place upon the Gentiles they were certain that the same Spirit and baptism had been imparted. Likewise after Paul had laid his hands upon the twelve Ephesians, he and those with him knew their prayer was answered and the Spirit was given when they heard them speak with tongues and prophesy.

The gift of tongues is a gift given after the baptism has occurred, and is as much of a gift as the gift of healing, or of discernment, and like them can be controlled, and used, or not used, as the person wills, for "the spirits of the prophets are subject to the prophets." But the speaking in the tongue as it occurs when the Spirit falls and the full baptism is imparted cannot be controlled and must run its course until the Spirit has fulfilled His work of baptizing the individual. It is very interesting to watch the Spirit's operations as the process of receiving the baptism takes place. Before the Spirit has overcome all resistance in the flesh and the mind, the utterances are but sounds, vowels or syllables, often repeated over and over again. As the power of God increases and the Spirit takes still greater possession these become words and phrases, and when the full baptism and infilling arrives the words in the unknown tongue roll forth in a torrent continuing for as much as several hours.

This measure of the Spirit which produces the clear utterance in the tongue, brings a satisfaction to the one hungry for God, and a continuous indwelling presence of the Spirit which no experience short of it can compare with. It also rouses all the latent powers in the person and puts them at the command and disposal of the Holy Spirit in a far greater measure than any lesser experience can. The speaking with the tongue does not bring the Spirit or the baptism, but the Spirit brings the tongue, and the clear speaking in the tongue is the indication that the Spirit is there, and that He has been yielded to, and has assumed control, more so than He has ever done before in that person. The speaking in the tongue becomes the evidence to the person and to others that the Spirit has moved in. And this evidence is biblical because it agrees with what happened to the apostles and was prevalent in the early church. So when the power of the Spirit comes upon a person in such a measure that he speaks in the tongue as the Spirit gives utterance he knows that the same experience and phenomenon has come upon him, and also the same baptism has arrived as came upon the one hundred and twenty and they of Cornelius' household.

The clear speaking in the tongue which occurs at the baptism may not occur again, but the power of 'the Spirit remains. Or it may dwindle to a few utterances or words during prayer or praise, but the measure of the anointing and the power that arrived when it first came forth still continues or even increases. Most persons who have received the apostolic baptism usually have a few utterances in tongues that come forth at times when the Spirit is more than normally felt. At times of special infillings and anointings they may speak in tongues as clearly and powerfully as when the original baptism came.

The uninterpreted speaking in the tongue is of little value in the congregation as far as general edification is concerned, and by Paul is discouraged. The use of the tongue during private worship is of great blessing and edification, and by Paul is encouraged and wished upon them all. But it is in the speaking in the *Satan* tongue as the Spirit gives utterance, such as *Hates* takes place at the receiving of the baptism, that the speaking in the tongue assumes its highest value and becomes of greatest importance. If this manifestation is the sign that the apostolic measure of the baptism has taken place, and such seems to be the evidence of the Scriptures and also from the history of the early church, then we can account for the reason why it is so universally fought against and belittled. If there is anything that Satan hates it is the Spirit-baptized members of the body of Christ. For it is thru them that God does His greatest works and Satan receives His greatest defeats and injury. The less there are of these folks the better his cause prospers. No wonder that he hates them and does all in his power to prevent others from obtaining the same measure of the Spirit's presence and anointing. If the full apostolic measure of the Spirit is not imparted until the speaking with tongues as the Spirit gives utterance occurs, then it is Satan's business to prevent hungry souls from pressing on until that measure of the Spirit arrives which brings forth the speaking in the tongue. To this end he belittles this manifestation and does all in his power to ridicule both it and all those who have experienced it. He wants hungry people to be satisfied with an experience far short of it, and this he has gotten thousands of ministers and laymen alike to accept.

Cause of Opposition Why is it that so many are so bitterly opposed to this manifestation? Is it possible that they realize their own lack, but are too proud and stubborn to acknowledge it in their own hearts, and then before others must justify the leanness of their souls by belittling the greater blessing and those more blessed? Such a stand is hypocritical to say the least, and will work untold damage both for time and eternity upon the one practicing it. Or is it that some have willfully allowed Satan to blind their eyes? They are ignorant because they desire to be ignorant, and because of this willful ignorance their ideas and conceptions are colored by their already preconceived notions. One thing is certain: no person needs to remain ignorant of the truth in this matter very long. Any person that will humbly ask God for light on this subject will soon receive it. Jesus says "If any man willeth to do His will, he shall know of the teaching, whether it be of God," and never was this saying any more true than in this case.

CHAPTER XVII

THE GIFT OF INTERPRETATION

As the operation of this gift is by necessity always associated with speaking with tongues and in a lesser degree with prophecy, considerable mention of it has already been made in former chapters. A few random and general remarks may, however, be of benefit:

Follows Baptism The gift of interpretation, like speaking with tongues, never is given until the full apostolic baptism has taken place. Consequently no one who has not received the full baptism can ever in the Spirit interpret a message spoken in tongues. All manifestations of the Spirit require great yieldance in order to come forth in purity, but none requires it any more than this one, because in this manifestation the thoughts of the mind must be completely set aside for the time being while the Spirit speaks. In order to be used by the Spirit as an instrument of interpretation, a person must be in a state of even greater yieldance than is necessary to receive the baptism. So any degree of yieldance less than is necessary to receive the baptism never will allow interpretation to come forth.

Unlocks Mysteries This gift is that operation of the Holy Spirit which unlocks the mysteries spoken by Him in tongues. And in order that these mysteries be revealed, Paul admonished, "Wherefore let him that speaketh in a tongue pray that he may interpret." I Cor. 14:13. The operation of this gift makes intelligible those mysteries and utterances which are not understood and which are of no value in the congregation as a whole. So the gift of interpretation is necessary in conjunction with the speaking in the tongue and the two operate together. Without interpretation the tongue is not to be used in the congregation. "If any man speaketh in a tongue; . . . and let one interpret: but if there be no interpreter, let him keep silence in the church." 1 Cor. 14: 27-28.

In its operation this manifestation is very much like the highest forms of prophecy in that it is in a language that is understood by the one speaking and those listening. And sometimes when prophecy and interpretation are intermingled it is difficult to tell one from the other.

Most of those who have received the full baptism speak in tongues more or less, but only a few interpret. It might be better if there were more. Paul recommends asking for this gift, and when this is done in a spirit of humility it usually is given. Some may receive it several years after the baptism.

All three of these kindred manifestations, prophecy, speaking with tongues, and interpretation, are brought about by a powerful presence of the Holy Spirit. This presence brings a feeling of wonderful spiritual ecstasy and so far as the flesh is concerned the sensations are much the same. Many seek the operation of this gift because of desiring these sensations, and often become out of God's order and grieve the Spirit by producing them in the strength of their own flesh and mind. No gift should be used for personal gratification.

Altho the audible part of the gift of interpretation is so like that of prophecy as to be hardly distinguishable as far as the audience is concerned, its operation upon the one exercised is often vastly different. The one who has this gift can often feel in advance when a message in tongues is about to come forth. If the Spirit is mightily present he may even in special cases receive the interpretation before the message in tongues is given. He then may pray that the tongues come forth, and when they have done so he gives it out. This usually produces a very powerful and edifying manifestation. Quite often if several interpreters are present they all can feel this and in a measure give the interpretation, but only one will receive the power and anointing to give it out. The one who gives the message in the tongue can usually tell if the interpretation is correct. The one who has given the message in the tongue feels bound or under restraint until the interpretation has come forth, and on its being given experiences a relief and a feeling of satisfaction. The one whom the Spirit chooses to interpret usually feels the power of the Spirit come mightily upon him while the message in tongues is being spoken and especially towards its close finds it almost impossible to remain silent.

Imparted Differently   The Spirit has several ways of imparting the interpretation. Sometimes the person who is to interpret will feel the power of the Spirit come upon him exceedingly strong and at the same time hear as it were a voice speaking within,

THE GIFT OF INTERPRETATION

repeating some sentence or phrase over and over. If the person then utters these words the Spirit will give more, the person listening to the voice inside and then uttering them with his mouth. This continues until the message is complete. This voice is not in the mind but in the inward parts. Something dwelling within does the speaking. This differs somewhat from prophecy in that in prophecy the Spirit will take control of the vocal organs and do the speaking Himself, while here He tells what is to be said and the person himself does the speaking. It is very evident that the mind is not drawn upon as very often the facts brought out in the interpreted message will be directly opposite to the interpreter's own opinion on the subject. Care must be exercised to keep the thoughts of the mind out, as any mental insertion will break the working of the Spirit and the message ceases. If the mind does enter it can be felt instantly by the one speaking and especially by those listening, who note a jar or break in the presence of the power of God. When the power of God is working any mental interpretation produces a discord. At one instance a message in tongues was given and after a few moments a man arose and gave the interpretation. It came slowly and deliberately and with many pauses but without any power upon himself or the audience. Even while he was speaking the power of the Spirit came upon another sitting by, but who refrained from saying anything, but at last was literally compelled to give it out and a powerful and very edifying message came forth. Then both the one who had spoken first and the audience realized that the first message was not the true interpretation, greatly humbling the speaker and becoming a valuable lesson to him and the others.

Powerful interpretations are about equal to prophecy. Consequently at times it may happen that the one interpreting may go on and give a prophetic message following the interpretation. However, this must not be expected or sought for as it may bring great confusion. And this will cause it. There are those who will go on speaking after the interpreting anointing has left them and call it prophecy, when it is nothing other than the ramblings and prattlings of their own mind.

Often Prophetic   At times the one who brings the interpretation sees a changing vision, which described becomes the message. One man as he felt the power to interpret come upon him, saw a parched, sun-baked sand, and in it an apparently dead, wilted plant. A stream of water commenced to flow, and on reaching the plant it revived, its leaves became green, a stalk shot up, a bud came, then a beautiful flower, and at last the ripened and well matured seed. Thus the message became a prophetic utterance. The one interpreting may feel that he is speaking directly to someone without knowing who this is. A young man in the ministry felt hedged about by insurmountable obstacles, and was much discouraged and greatly puzzled to know the outcome of certain pending conditions. The way seemed closed with no way to turn. An interpretation given by another became a direct message to him telling him what to do and how things would work out. He himself felt the voice of God speaking direct to his own soul. Things worked out just as the message had said. No one in the audience or the one interpreting knew whom the message was for.

THE GIFT OF INTERPRETATION

The prophetic message requires far more power to break forth than the interpreted one, and for this reason is more effective. It seems that the message in tongues coming forth in power clears the air and paves the way for the interpretation. It is noticed at times that if the message in tongues is weak, the interpretation is the same. If the message in tongues is strong and powerful the interpretation will also be sharp and effective.

The interpreted message may be a rebuke to individuals, whether saint or sinner, or to the assembly as a whole. Or it may be an appeal to the unsaved. Often at the close of a powerful evangelistic message the Spirit may give a message in tongues with its interpretation which becomes a direct warning and appeal to the unconverted. If all flesh can be eliminated this is very effective towards breaking down opposition and melting stony hearts.

Often Misused But this gift, or rather its counterfeit, may be misused. The thoughts and ideas of men are often given as the word of the Lord, causing confusion and disgust. Unscrupulous persons may use this as a means of fostering false doctrines, unclean practices and even sin. But both the false message and the false messenger can easily be detected and discerned by anyone walking close to the Lord, so the danger is not as great as it might appear to be.

CHAPTER XVIII

The Gift of Healing

An Operation of the Holy Spirit   The healing of the body thru the prayer of faith or the laying on of hands in the name of Jesus is primarily an operation of the Holy Spirit. Possibly no other manifestation of the Spirit has been as effective in opening the way for the preaching of the Word and the spreading of the Gospel as this one. In the early church days it proved the name of Jesus to be greater than that of any of the gods of Egypt, Greece or Rome. To-day it effectively opens the doors to the hearts of the heathen who find that the power of God in delivering them from the miseries of bodily ailments is greater than that of their own demon-possessed priests and exorcists.

Altho the greatest working of this manifestation is in the New Testament time, we do find some mention of it in the Old Testament also. Very probably the phenomenon was not as pronounced in those early days as it became later, but nevertheless it existed. In Exodus 15:26 we read: "If thou wilt diligently hearken to the voice of Jehovah thy God, and wilt do that which is right in his eyes, and wilt give ear to his commandments, and keep all his statutes, I will put none of the diseases upon thee, which I have put upon the Egyptians: for I am Jehovah that healeth thee." Here Jehovah calls Himself a God who heals and He would hardly take these attributes to Himself unless He was both capable of healing and did heal. The promise here seems in a way to be the form of a prevention of disease. He not only could remove the disease after it came, but He also had the power to prevent it from arriving in the first place. But the promise *In* is conditional: "If thou wilt hearken . . . *Old* and wilt do . . . and wilt give ear . . . *Testament* and keep statutes," then "I will put none of the diseases upon thee." God knows the mechanism of the human body and its relation towards disease and by ordering their manner of living could put them in such condition that their bodies would have the strength to resist most diseases. We to-day might learn much from this. Without a doubt our present civilization in many ways is against nature, both in foods eaten and in acquired habits and customs, all of which combine to lower the body's vitality and its protection against preventable disease. But God's power can be a powerful and preventative check upon the germination and spread of these bacteria and organisms which are the cause of such pestilences as smallpox, influenza, typhoid fever, and the like. These promises seem to have been very effective upon the Hebrews, both in the Old Testament times and to-day, for the Jews have proved to be a very strong, keen, aggressive and healthy race.

In the one hundred and third Psalm we read:

> "Bless Jehovah, O my soul,
> And forget not all his benefits."

And then among the benefits mentioned we find this one:

"Who healeth all thy diseases."

Some have tried to spiritualize this verse, as they also do other verses that disagree with their ideas and theories, by saying that it does not have reference to the body, but rather to spiritual desires and needs. In the other four benefits mentioned ample provision is made for forgiving iniquity, redeeming from destruction, crowning with mercies, and satisfying the desire with good things. It means all diseases and nothing else.

The prophet Isaiah who over seven hundred years before the time saw the "Anointed One" and so wonderfully pictured Him, cried thus, "Surely he hath borne our griefs, and carried our sorrows." Isaiah 53:4. And this Matthew quotes, saying, "And when even was come, they brought unto him many possessed with demons: and he cast out the spirits with a word, and healed all that were sick: that it might be fulfilled which was spoken thru Isaiah the prophet, saying, Himself took our infirmities, and bare our diseases." Matt. 8:16-17.

In the Atonement Thru causing the fall of man, Satan has brought evil into the world, bringing sin upon the whole race, disease upon our bodies and a curse upon the very vegetation. This evil with all its progeny, Christ came to remove and undo, for He was manifest to set at nought the works of the devil. So Christ became a curse for our sakes and upon the cross He bore the whole curse resting upon man and all creation. Thru His death and resurrection He hath redeemed us and with us all creation also, all of which shall be revealed in its season.

THE GIFT OF HEALING

The provision for this was made thru Calvary, but that which was provided is not yet as fully available to humanity and creation as a whole as it shall be later. Sin and death are still here and "the whole creation groaneth and travaileth in pain together until now." Rom. 8:22. But to them who now believe, the blood of Christ is available and operative for cleansing from the guilt of sin and also the power of it. In the fullness of time, this mortal shall put on immortality and this corruptible incorruption, and the power of death and the grave shall be broken.

The Age to Come This provision thru the atonement shall become fully available in the age to come. Even the creation shall be freed from its present bondage because Christ in the crown of thorns bore its curse on the cross. In that age when the power of God shall be universally present and all nations shall see the glory of God, the knowledge of the Lord shall cover the earth as the waters cover the sea and salvation shall be so widespread and common that a sinner a hundred years old shall be accursed. Then the plowman shall follow the reaper. Because of the freedom from disease thru the presence of God's Spirit who then will hold in check those agents that now cause it, man's allotted time will not be threescore and ten, as it now is, but will be as the age of trees, or hundreds of years.

This same Spirit who will then work so wonderfully, is now present, and altho checked in His operations by the power of Satan and this awful age of unbelief, He can, and does, and is able to make operative upon us now, at least some of those provisions made thru Christ upon the cross. Paul prayed that the Ephesians might receive among other things, "a spirit of wisdom and revelation in the knowledge of him," and that they might know "what is the exceeding greatness of his power to us-ward who believe, according to that working of the strength of his might, which he wrought in Christ, when he raised him from the dead." Eph. 1:17-20. In other words he was anxious that they might know how mighty is the power of God toward His saints to reveal and make known and operative those things which God has provided for them in Christ Jesus. And among other things, one of these is healing for our bodies.

Available There are two statements in the New Tes-
Now tament dealing with healing and these are as clear, definite and straight to the point as any covering salvation. If we accept those promises made concerning redemption from sin and apply them to ourselves and our age and time, then why quibble over those on healing and assign them to former ages and past generations? If we accept the promises made for salvation as operative to-day, which they are, as demonstrated daily in the salvation of souls, then why not accept the other as for to-day also, especially as we see and hear of those whose faith God honors to the healing of their bodies?

One of these promises is in James. "Is any among you sick? let him call for the elders of the church; and let them pray over him, anointing him with oil in the name of the Lord: and the prayer of faith shall save him that is sick, and the Lord shall raise him up; and if he have committed sins, it shall be forgiven him.

THE GIFT OF HEALING

Confess therefore your sins one to another, and pray one for another, that ye may be healed. The supplication of a righteous man availeth much in its working." James 5:14-16.

A
Definite
Promise

If any promise is plain, this one is. The conditions and instructions to be followed are very definite and concise. If any man is sick, then let that sick man call for the elders of the church. Evidently any man of faith will do, and elders usually are such individuals. Then the elders are to come at this request and perform certain duties. They anoint the sick one with oil, not in their own name or in that of some teacher of religion or church, but in the name of the Lord. As no special variety or kind of oil is mentioned they are at liberty to use any at hand, with a possible preference for olive oil. After having prayed the prayer of faith over the sick one they have done their duty and the rest remains with God. "And the prayer of faith shall save him that is sick, and the Lord shall raise him up."

In order that the conditions of this promise be fulfilled the prayer of faith is necessary. The very fact that the sick one calls for the elders shows that he believes in a measure at least. It has happened in instances that the elders themselves have had no faith, but that God has worked anyway, honoring the faith of the sick one. There have been instances in which friends of the sick one have had faith and have called for the elders who also have had faith, while the one sick has had neither faith nor unbelief, just a willingness to take whatever came, and God has honored by healing. But

Meet
Conditions

there are those who have experimented with this promise, just to see if it would work, rather expecting that it would not, and of course nothing has happened. And then there are others who have both anointed and prayed without any request having been made either by the sick one or his friends or relatives, and the conditions not being met, nothing has happened. This ordinance of the church is not to be peddled around promiscuously by such as have no other desire in the use of it than to extol their own gifts and powers.

But why not believe this promise and make use of it? The first thing a sick person now does is to run for the physician, and let us thank God for the physicians that those who lack faith can fall back on. But why should it not be as common and customary to call for a few faithful servants of the Lord first, and let God show His power and get glory for Himself that we and others might come to know Him better? The average Christian home is in many instances a miniature apothecary's shop and after all the liniments, lotions, salves and pills have failed and the physician says that there is no hope, then God is called on as a last resort. Why not call God first?

A woman belonging to a very respectable church in a California city was told by the physicians that she had a cancer. All tests and reactions gave this indication. A portion removed showed cancer tissue. Her relatives, friends and the several physicians strongly advised a surgical operation as the only means of saving her life. Unwillingly she consented, but first demanded that the elders of the church come and pray for her, fulfilling this promise in James 5:14-15. The evening before she was to be operated upon they anointed and prayed for her. The next morning when the assembled surgeons were to go to work upon her they could find no cancer or trace of it. They were astonished, to say the least, but could offer no explanation. God had fulfilled His promise.

In this scripture no promise is made as to when the Lord will perform this. The inference is that the Lord will commence to undertake immediately, either resulting in instant deliverance or gradual improvement as the case may be.

In the great commission in Mark 16:15-18, the Lord said, "Go ye into all the world, and preach the gospel to the whole creation. He that believeth and is baptized shall be saved; . . . And these signs shall accompany them that believe: in my name shall they cast out demons; . . . they shall lay hands on the sick, and they shall recover." Many whose faith is not as it should be have tried by various methods to explain away this passage. When the destructive higher critics tried to undermine the value and steadfastness of the Word of God, they explained that certain undesirable verses, passages and books were written in, or left out, or were the product of some other author. Later researches have proved them wrong. Is it not peculiar that when some people's theology and lives do not agree with some scripture they stoop to the same methods? Even tho that passage never had been recorded, its truths would still stand because those signs did follow in the early church and do follow to-day when faith and the power of the Holy Spirit are present. This ordinance of laying on of hands for the healing of the sick was much practiced in the early church. Sometimes the one prayed for was anointed with oil and sometimes not.

For Us Now — Many have tried to limit this phenomenon to apostolic and early church times. In His great commission the Lord commanded them to go into all the world. It was absolutely impossible for those to whom He directly spoke to do this. So the commission was not to them alone but unto all the church, which includes that portion of it alive to-day. He added that those who believed and were baptized would be saved and this certainly was not limited to that time only, for those who believe and are baptized to-day experience salvation now as well as those who believed and were baptized then. And certain signs would follow the believer. Which believer? Only those who heard and accepted the apostles' personal message, or only those who believed in the first few centuries? If the commission is to the whole church during the whole church age, and salvation is to all believers during the whole age, then the signs upon the believers are for the whole age also and that includes to-day. Then why do not the signs follow to-day? They do, when real living faith and the power of the Spirit are present in a person's life. The very fact that the signs do not follow as generally now as was common in the early church is the greatest evidence of the present-day decadence and lack of power among God's people, and one of the reasons why so little at present is being accomplished in the way of salvation of souls, and why the general tendency seems to be that of having a form of godliness but denying the power thereof.

It was the power of the Spirit which operated thru Stephen who "full of grace and power, wrought great wonders and signs among the people." Acts 6:8. It was the operations of the signs and especially healing

THE GIFT OF HEALING

which opened the door for Philip's preaching in Samaria, for "The multitudes gave heed with one accord unto the things that were spoken by Philip, when they heard, and saw the signs which he did . . . and many that were palsied, and that were lame, were healed." Acts 8:6-7. Without a doubt if these things could happen in the church to-day the gospel cause and the work of the Lord as a whole would not be in the position that it now is.

The gift of healing has been given to the church as a whole as a common possession, and the privilege to anoint with oil and lay on the hands is given to each member of it, but the special anointing of the Spirit for healing is not common to every member. As Paul says, "Are all workers of miracles? have all gifts of healings?" 1 Cor. 12:29-30. The Spirit in "dividing to each one severally even as he will," 1 Cor. 12:11, has in His wisdom found some who have greater faith and can better lend themselves to this gift than others.

This gift, like the lesser forms of prophecy and the less keen forms of discernment, can exist previous to receiving the full baptism. It above all things requires great faith and with it keen discernment, and the more of both, the more effectively the person possessing it lends himself to its operation. The receiving of the baptism imparts much of each and therefore increases the working of the gift very considerably.

All operations of the Spirit in ridding the body of disease, ailments or deformities, can rightly be called healing. But the Scripture seems to consider miracles or powers as a greater manifestation and classifies it as such. Possibly the lesser manifestation, such as the relieving from disease and the lesser discomforts is called healing, while that of instantaneous curing of deformities and the casting out of demons is called miracles or powers.

Works   The gift of healing may produce either a
Differently complete instantaneous result, or a change resulting in a gradual betterment or restoration. In Jesus' ministry one individual commenced to amend at that very hour. John 4:52. A tubercular Indian, much emaciated, unable to eat or sleep, was brought into a meeting and prayed for before the service commenced. She fell asleep while being prayed for and slept during the whole service. She slept all that night and the next day ate five meals, and continued at this rate for several weeks, increasing in health and strength. A woman had been practically a nervous invalid for sixteen years, with months at a time spent in hospitals and over three thousand dollars spent in physicians' fees. She was very thin, had little or no strength, and was unable to sleep without the use of drugs. She arose at nine A. M., retired again at two P. M. for several hours, then at night at eight. She could do only the least fatiguing part of her housework, while her husband and boys and hired help or neighbors did the rest. Washing, scrubbing and ironing were out of the question. On being prayed for once she slept well that night, but the next night did not. Being prayed for the second time she slept well for two nights, and the third could not. The third time she was prayed for she slept well every evening for almost a week. These successions of praying and betterments covered about a month. In less than two months she had gained much in flesh, slept well, did all

THE GIFT OF HEALING

her housework and had much time to spare for the work of the Lord. At this writing, eight years later, she is still well and robust, and praises God for deliverance. This resulted in the salvation of practically her whole family.

In diseases such as influenza, tuberculosis, typhoid fever and the like, which are caused by the working and effect of some bacteria or germ, the power of God in some cases seems to kill the germ instantly and then allow the natural forces of the body to restore health and strength. Or in cases where the body forces are not great enough to combat the germ and its toxins, or poisons, the power of the Spirit may supply that needed strength so that they can, and the healing proceeds in the natural way. This more often happens when the ordinance in James 5:14-15 is used.

In the laying on of hands, the one praying and the one prayed for feel the power of God, and this almost invariably brings a definite and pronounced result for the better. A forty-five-year-old woman was sick with what the physicians diagnosed as pneumonia. For five days the "case" ran its normal course with the usual fever, congestion and other symptoms. On the sixth day the woman was prayed for, both anointed and hands laid on. Shortly afterwards the physician made his call and to his astonishment could find no fever or other symptoms aside from weakness which in a few days left. He stated that according to all medical tests and knowledge she had a well developed case of pneumonia, and that for days it had gone on as such, but that suddenly in some way that he did not understand, it had been checked and the woman to all intents had become well.

Salvation Sometimes when anointing with oil, and
Accompanies usually when hands are laid on, the one
prayed for feels the power of the Spirit
go thru the afflicted part or possibly the whole body.
This usually brings a soothing sensation which drives
out the pain and eases any discomforts. This power
at times may be so pronounced that the person becomes
like one intoxicated or in special cases even helpless.
When the person is unsaved, the coming of the power
brings salvation. Disease and sin in some way seem
linked together and when the power of God drives out
the one the other goes also. One person had come some
sixty miles to be anointed and prayed for, which was
done. As hands were laid on, the power of the Spirit
came and was felt. But on being questioned the answer
was, "I am still sick, but feel so glad and happy." Those
praying hardly understood what to make of it, but
prayed again, when the power of the Spirit again came,
and healing took place. The person then related that
at the first instance salvation had come, and at the second healing. In order for the power of God to flow
thru the body the person must be yielded, and when a
person is willing to yield, salvation is not far away. It
may be possible that God in some instances allows sickness to come in order that stubborn wills be bent and
the yieldance be brought about that opens the way for
salvation.

Yielding The more a person can yield, the more
Necessary freely the power of God can flow, and consequently the greater the results and the
more complete the healing. Some people are naturally
resistive to any influence of God or man, and such are

THE GIFT OF HEALING

hard to pray for and most often feel but little of the power of God, or none at all, and all too commonly are not healed. A saved person is on the average more receptive to the Spirit than one unsaved, and one who has received the baptism still more so. Unless some sin or other hindrance is in the way one who has the baptism usually gets healed.

At times when the power of the Spirit is present, healing comes much more readily than at other times. We find that in one instance in Jesus' ministry "the power of the Lord was with Him to heal." Luke 5:17. God's presence brings added faith and with unbelief removed, the Spirit has freer course. At the close of a revival campaign in a church where large numbers had been saved, a request was made for a talk on healing. At the end of the last service this talk was given and some eighteen or twenty crowded forward to be prayed for. Every one felt the power of God and some were instantly healed, while with others it came a day or two later. Some months later inquiry was made which disclosed that as far as could be found everyone was healed.

Most usually when hands are laid on, the one prayed for feels something akin to an electric current pass thru his body. The one praying at the same time feels something of the same nature flow out from him thru the arms and the hands. This can be so powerful as to leave the hands and arms numb and without feeling. Very probably this is the same as, or related to what, Jesus experienced when the woman with the issue of blood slipped behind Him and touched the hem of His garment, for He said, "Some one did touch Me; for I perceived that power had gone forth from Me." Luke

8:46: This is very pronounced in the ministry of those that the Lord uses for healing. It is even more pronounced in the casting out of demons, which matter will be dealt with later. In fact, it seems that the possession of the gift of healing is dependent upon the possession of this virtue or power, and the more of it a person has the more effective is his ministry. The degree and measure in which this virtue and power of the Spirit can flow forth is dependent upon several things, including: the general presence of the Spirit of God, the measure of the healer's anointing, the degree of yieldance in the one prayed for, and the degree of health, or freshness, of the one doing the praying.

Virtue Flows Out

If the Holy Spirit is powerfully present in a meeting this virtue flows more freely than if the meeting is tight, under which last condition at times it may not flow at all. After a powerful evangelistic service in which the Spirit is heavy upon the service, or when a spirit of praise is resting, people are more easily healed than otherwise. If a spirit of expectancy fills the atmosphere and a special service is set aside for healing, the Spirit will most usually be found present to heal.

One who is used in healing finds that if he is "prayed up" and has the anointing upon his own life, this power comes forth much more readily than if he is too busy with secular things to take time to pray or wait upon the Lord.

Another very determining factor is the degree of surrender in the one prayed for. If sin is in the way or a rebelliousness towards God exists, the Spirit never flows forth until these are removed or repented of. Under these conditions the one praying can sometimes feel the power or virtue flow out as far as his hands and there stop, not passing into the body of the other. Some persons' minds are naturally resistive and while awake cannot yield, but if prayed for while asleep can be healed. The presence of a demon up to a certain point can hinder the flowing forth of the healing power, but if thru the spirit of discernment this presence is detected and rebuked, the power of God will, like an overwhelming flood, drive out both him and the disease.

Produces Tiredness The flowing out of this virtue seems to drain the resources of the body in some way. The source does not appear to be in the mind but rather in the inward parts. When drawn upon too often or too close together it leaves the person weak and exceedingly tired, with a sensation of severe internal emptiness. Those much used in prayer for the sick often become so tired as to be unable to stand. If drawn upon too frequently without sufficient time for recuperation, nervous exhaustion may result. When rested and in normal condition this healing power flows forth far more readily than when tired or sick.

But healing thru prayer and the operation of the Holy Spirit is not always dependent upon either anointing with oil or the laying on of hands. A request for prayer may come by wire, or mail, or a word-of-mouth messenger. When prayer is made the sick one, tho miles away, may feel the power of the Spirit pass thru the body, bringing deliverance. This happened in Jesus' ministry when the nobleman's son was healed, and also when the demon was driven out of the Syrophoenician woman's daughter. A man was threatened with incipient insanity and sent word twenty-five hundred miles

Works at a Distance

for prayer. At the very hour that prayer was made, twenty-five hundred miles away, he felt the presence of the Spirit come into the room and upon him. Some parents had a six or eight-months-old child, born with a deformed back which medical aid professed inability to help. The father sent a written request and prayer was made. Two days later the father himself came to report that as far as could be discerned the babe's back had become normal.

If a person has the baptism, and it may happen in other instances also, his own prayer for healing may cause the power of God to pass thru the afflicted part, causing healing. A young man while cutting timber in the mountains, thru dampness and cramped position had contracted something in his limbs that was exceedingly painful and felt like acute muscular rheumatism. It became so severe that it was with difficulty that he could be on his feet, and it was too painful to walk more than one hundred feet without a rest. He asked God to heal and instantly felt the power of God pass thru his limbs from the hips downward and completely remove all pain. In less than an hour afterwards he walked over a mile without any sense of discomfort.

During the influenza epidemic a young man was taken ill and put to bed, with all the indications of the disease. Medical aid was offered, but refused. He told the Lord that he was perfectly willing to die if his time had come, but added that his family and the work of the Lord needed his presence a while longer. In about fifteen minutes he felt the power of the Spirit come upon him so mightily that he went into a trance, lasting for some time, and saw the Lord. On regaining consciousness every pain and discomfort was gone,

THE GIFT OF HEALING

and for several days afterwards he felt an unusual presence of the power of God upon his flesh and a peculiar sensation of lightness, freedom and strength.

Or it may happen that even without any request being made, when the power of the Spirit is powerfully present healing may come to afflicted ones. In a revival campaign in a Baptist church, at the close of a powerful meeting and while a heavy spirit of conviction was resting upon the audience, a woman was struck by the power of God and suddenly began to sing in the Spirit. Later she testified that at that moment she was healed in her body. Another, while in a meeting when God's power was manifest, began to weep for joy and then publicly stated that while sitting there her eyesight, poor for years and requiring heavy glasses, suddenly seemed cleared, and there demonstrated that at an arm's length she could read the finest print. Trees that before even with the glasses seemed but a mass of green, now to the naked eyesight became leaves and branches.

CHAPTER XIX

MIRACLES AND POWERS—PART I

Any unusual thing with the cause unknown is called a miracle. As soon as the cause is known it becomes commonplace. Many of the things which to-day are so common and generally in use that our civilization depends upon them, at one time were classed as miracles and held in awe by all. When the first reports of such discoveries and inventions as the telegraph, the telephone, the Rontgen rays and radio were circulated, many called them miracles and others were exceedingly skeptical, and still others ridiculed the idea that any such things could be. All because they did not understand the underlying principles and forces. Later these people, becoming more acquainted with facts, made use of these very things which they themselves had denied could exist.

Man's Opinion Many to-day are skeptical about, deny and laugh at, the possibility of biblical, or modern miracles, just because they are in ignorance of what causes them, the power of God or the Holy Spirit. This Spirit or power which they deny or are ignorant of, is just as real and more powerful than any of the forces or powers that underlie our inventions and civilization.

To the man of the jungle, the phonograph, the telephone, the electric light and the airplane are mysteries unfathomable. When he sees them he knows they exist, but cannot explain why or how they operate, so he calls them "strong medicine," "witchcraft" and the like. The unbelieving learned man stands in somewhat the same relation to the power of God. He denies that the biblical records of miracles are true, or if he sees anything of the same nature to-day he calls it hypnotism, psychological phenomena or just plain "humbug." So the jungle man and the unbelieving learned man are in the same boat. The one is ignorant of what underlies and causes the products of civilization, and the other of the operation of God's Spirit.

This ignorance concerning the power of God is the cause of the prevalent spirit of unbelief, both inside and outside of the church. This is why so many of the theological students and preachers of to-day do not believe, and are at a loss to explain such recorded incidents as Daniel's visions, the three Hebrews in the fiery furnace, the raising of Lazarus and the resurrection of the Lord. These are impossible as far as the natural is concerned, and as long as man knows of nothing beyond the natural they are unexplainable. And the spiritually unexplainable the natural mind most easily gets away from by saying that it never happened or does not exist. However, when we take into consideration the Spirit of God, the force that created the universe and now holds it together, the recorded incidents are no longer mysteries but simply a record of His operations.

God But why should a miracle be considered improb-
Can able? If God's power in the beginning brought the visible universe and the invisible angelic

hosts and the principalities and powers in the heavenly places into being, has it since in any way decreased? Is He not now just as able to create as He then was, or can He not now if necessary rearrange the relation of created things toward each other? If God has created and maintains the elements that make up a bone in a human body and has laid down the laws that govern its formation, growth and nourishment, is not God also capable of healing that bone or even creating a new one if it be His pleasure? Most assuredly He can.

Learned men tell us that all matter is electrical in its origin and structure. They have found the smallest indivisible form of any element to be an atom. But they have also found that the atom itself is composed of something still smaller, namely, a central positive charge of electricity surrounded by one or more rapidly moving and revolving negative electric charges. All the atoms of the same element are alike, but the atoms of the different elements differ from each other. All atoms of iron are the same, and all atoms of copper are the same, and all atoms of oxygen are the same, but the atoms of iron, copper and oxygen differ from each other. And this relation holds true to the limits of the visible universe. The positive charge of electricity and the revolving electrons, or negative charges, are the same and their relation to each other is the same in all the atoms of the same element. But the positive charge varies with the element. The electrons are the same in all elements, but their number and relation to the central positive charge is different in each element. The heavier the element, the heavier are its atoms. And the heavier the atom, the stronger is its central positive charge, and in turn the number of electrons revolving

MIRACLES AND POWERS, PART I

around it. An atom of hydrogen has a central positive electric charge of one unit of strength and around this revolves one charge of negative electricity or electron. An atom of helium has a positive charge of four units of strength and around this revolves four electrons. An atom of oxygen has a positive charge of sixteen units of strength and sixteen electrons. An atom of iron has a positive charge of fifty-six units of strength and fifty-six electrons. And this same arrangement holds true with all the elements. The mutual attraction between the central charge and the revolving electrons is so great that they are practically inseparable except at a tremendous outlay of energy.

Just what carries these electrical charges no one has satisfactorily explained. Some say the "ether" but no one seems to know what the ether is. Nor has anyone yet explained where these electric charges came from originally, or by what power these electrons were set into such a tremendous state of motion or revolution. We all know the first great law of dynamics to be the fact that all energy must come from energy, and that there is no such thing as getting power from nothing, and therefore the impossibility of "perpetual motion." But where did this tremendous energy, electrical in form, which so mysteriously manifests itself as matter and the elements, and constitutes the whole visible creation, come from originally? It must have some source and beginning and who can that beginning be? And who originated and now maintains these wonderful brain-staggering laws that now govern their operation? Possibly Paul saw the answer when he stated, "For of him, and thru him, and unto him, are all things." Rom. 11:36. Or possibly the author of the book of Hebrews solved the riddle when he said, "God hath . . . spoken unto us in his Son, . . . thru whom also he made the worlds; . . . and upholding all things by the word of his power . . . " Heb. 1:1-3. Maybe Paul whispered the secret to the Colossians when he said, "All things have been created thru him, and unto him; and he is before all things, and in him all things consist (hold together)." Col. 1:16-17.

All Matter from God   Is it not possible and highly probable that these electrical charges represent a manifestation of God's power and that creation itself took place when thru the "Word" this power flowed forth bringing the elements into existence? Is it not possible that power still flows forth from God and that thru the Holy Spirit He maintains the whole visible creation and the laws that govern it? Is it not further possible that when creation has fulfilled its purpose of bringing into being a blood-redeemed and Spirit-filled people after God's own heart, that this outflow of energy and power may cease and all the elements disappear and end their existence, and God in His spirit form, and His eternal life possessing children with Him, alone remain?

The Spirit Is Able   If God's Spirit and power is the origin and the maintainer of matter, cannot then this same Spirit and power exercise control over matter whenever necessary and it is the will of God to do so? Why should it to-day seem impossible for God's power now to flow thru a human body and kill disease germs, touch the frayed ends of tired nerves, or counteract the effects of toxins and poisons in exhausted muscles? Can He not change the shape of an eyeball, clarifying the eyesight, touch and splice together the loose nerve connections in the brain and restore sanity, or by His power cause some special excitation of the glands, or nerve centers, so that teeth grow, bones straighten, or inoperative organs function correctly? Many believe that God can do these things in the course of time, but then why not in a few hours, minutes or seconds? At Lazarus' death and resurrection four days of decay in a hot climate had completely destroyed the blood and fluids of the body, and so corrupted the nerves, tissues and cells and changed the structure of the organs as to render them absolutely incapable of sustaining life. But at Jesus' "Lazarus, come forth!" the power of God in a few seconds restored what four days of decay had destroyed, killed the germs causing the decay and gave life to the dead body. Many persons, including some preachers, cannot believe the record of this miracle simply because they cannot explain it on scientific grounds. They fail to recognize the power and person of the Holy Spirit who thru Jesus Christ is the origin and maintainer of all creation.

Jesus had a special and practically limitless anointing of the Spirit and with it unlimited faith. Consequently there were no bounds upon the operation of the Spirit thru Him, except as determined by the faith of the people themselves. So most of His healings and wonders took the form of miracles and manifestations in which the power of God flowed forth thru Him and practically instantly produced the results desired. When He fed the five thousand His own faith in God set such a measure of the power of God in operation that bread and fish actually were created and this food created was exactly identical with what they already had on hand and contained exactly the same food elements as the other. It was real bread and fish, as it satisfied the people and the disciples gathered of the remains for their own use. When He walked on the sea the force of gravity was set aside as far as His own body was concerned and Peter's also as long as he had his eyes on the Lord. As long as Peter believed, the power of God sustained him. When his eyes and ears perceived the wind and the waves, and the unnaturalness of the whole situation dawned upon him, his faith failed. And when it did the power of the Spirit ceased to work. The force of gravity instantly claimed its own and down went Peter. When the Spirit ceased acting the miracle came to an end. Many unbelieving theologians try to give all manner of natural explanations for this event, all of which are ridiculous and clearly expose their lack of knowledge of God's power and Spirit. Just what happened is hard to say. But most probably either the power of God for a time set at nought the force of gravity or else actually lifted or sustained the bodies of Jesus and Peter.

Nor was the performing of miracles limited to Jesus' ministry. Peter and John, entering into the temple, saw the forty-year-old beggar, born lame, sitting at the temple gate and Peter said unto him, "Look on us . . . Silver and gold have I none; but what I have, that give I thee. In the name of Jesus Christ of Nazareth, walk. And he took him by the right hand, and raised him up: and immediately his feet and his ankle-bones received strength. And leaping up, he stood, and began to walk; and he entered with them into the temple, walking, and leaping, and praising God." Acts 3:4-8. When a man forty years old, born a cripple, in a few seconds of time has his bones straightened, and wasted and never used muscles suddenly are given life and strength so that he can walk and even leap, then some force and power not ordinarily operative or known has been at work. Scientifically such a thing is impossible and therefore disbelieved and ridiculed by many. But with God all things are possible thru the operation of His Spirit.

This same Spirit which was present in Jesus' ministry and later, is still here. What He has done in the past He can do now and does, when the necessary faith is present. It actually looks as tho Jesus' resurrection and ascension has paved the way for even greater manifestations of His power, for "greater works than these shall he do; because I go unto the Father." John 14:12.

The Same To-day   The power of God, as an immutable thing, can neither increase nor decrease. He is "all power" and knows no limitations as far as ability or possibilities are concerned, or except as hindered by unbelief. But the degree in which this "all power" can manifest itself is determined by various conditions and these conditions determine the measure in which it can flow forth and be set in motion. It really looks as tho the Spirit is always present, but that certain limiting factors and influences at times render Him inoperative and passive. He is always ready to work and when restrictions are removed, such as unbelief and others, He immediately becomes active and the degree of activity, and consequently the results, is determined by the liberty given. Unbelief is the devil's most powerful tool in binding the activity of God's Spirit. He started with it in the garden when he said, "Hath God said . . . ?" and has very successfully kept using it ever since. If all restrictions were removed there would be no limit to what the Spirit could and would accomplish. This property of the Spirit is as old as the Spirit Himself, and He is eternal. At Creation there was no unbelief and He worked untrammelled. In the days of old, such men as Abraham, Moses, Samuel, Elijah and the various prophets, and a faithful king or two, by their faith pushed back the then present unbelief, and He worked. In Jesus' ministry thru His immeasurable faith, but nevertheless at times hindered by the people's own hardness of heart, He did still greater things. And to-day He is still as powerful and capable of operating as He ever was before, and will operate when the necessary faith is there.

Faith is not a man-made product but cometh by hearing and is a gift of the Spirit. 1 Cor. 12:9. And this is given to the church as a whole, and more so, to such special individuals as the Spirit Himself may decide. Thru these individuals especially endued with faith God can and does work, and upon them the gift of miracles and powers rests. The fact that miracles and powers are scarce these days is not any indication of any lessening of power on God's part, but rather that but few persons will yield themselves sufficiently to God to allow the Holy Spirit to impart the necessary faith. The fault lies with man and not with God.

In the performing of miracles and powers the presence of the Spirit comes much more powerfully than in healings, both upon the one praying and the one that is prayed for. The work done takes place

Greater much more quickly, or even instantaneously.
Than Such happened in practically all of Jesus'
Healing healings and also with Philip's ministry in
Samaria and with Stephen. Likewise when Peter healed the lame man and when he said, "Aeneas, Jesus Christ healeth thee: arise, and make thy bed." Acts 9:34.

These powerful operations of the Spirit of God done in those days in the name of Jesus became very effective in attracting attention to Christ and consequently awakened an interest in this new religion. Peter, after healing the lame man, told the Jews, "And by faith in his name hath his name made this man strong, whom ye behold and know: yea, the faith which is thru him hath given him this perfect soundness in the presence of you all." Acts 3:16. People saw that there was something supernatural in it, and that this supernatural was connected with the name of Jesus. The curiosity then opened the way for the telling about His death and resurrection which is the gospel, and it in turn produced salvation.

The church thru losing the necessary faith has lost her miracle-working power. The pope at Rome was showing some visitors the treasures and valuables of the Vatican and remarked, "As you notice, we cannot say with Peter, 'Silver and gold have I none.'" "Yes," answered the other, "But neither can you say, 'Take up thy bed, and walk.'" And what is true in this instance is also too true in others. Not that miracles are not needed, for they certainly are. Nothing could be more effective in opening the eyes of the people to the existence of a living God and demonstrating the power of the gospel, than this powerful operation of the Spirit of God. And it may be that God will have to raise up persons thru whom He can thus work before this present spirit of lethargy and domination of the power of the devil will be broken.

Miracles Magnify Jesus It is noticeable that in New Testament times the great revivals always were preceded and accompanied by powerful healings and workings of the Spirit. When Philip was in Samaria "the multitudes gave heed with one accord unto the things that were spoken by Philip, when they heard, and saw the signs which he did." Acts 8:6. When Paul was in Ephesus the whole city was moved, "And God wrought special miracles by the hands of Paul: insomuch that unto the sick were carried away from his body handkerchiefs or aprons, and the diseases departed from them, and the evil spirits went out." Acts 19:11-12. "And the name of the Lord Jesus was magnified." "So mightily grew the word of the Lord and prevailed." Acts 19:17, 20. In our days some of the greatest stirs and awakenings in spiritual interest come thru the operation of miracles and healings. This attracts the attention of that class of unsaved, who, as a rule, are never seen inside of a church building. The operation of that something which they do not understand gets the best of their curiosity so they must come and see for themselves. And the more opposition that is aroused from medical men and a certain class of unregenerated theologians, the greater the interest. In not a few instances the marked healing of some one person has opened the way for salvation to come to others of the same family, or a whole blood relation. The healing of one woman resulted in the salvation of practically her whole family, relatives and many friends. From the healing of another the salvation of twenty-six others was traced.

Space forbids going any further into the subject, so the telling of but one instance will have to suffice to show that God is still able to do these things. A young man called to me from one of the upper windows of a fire-station where he was serving as a truck-driver. On getting to his room I found that his neck was swollen to an enormous size and so stiff that he could not turn his head. He was very weak and dizzy from toxic-poisoning and barely able to be on his feet. He told me that he had "quincy" and that a physician some hours before had said that unless a change came quickly for the better an operation would be necessary. It had swollen considerably since then and on examination I found the throat almost closed, leaving only a small hole barely large enough to admit the end of a lead pencil and that there was great danger of strangulation. He begged me to pray for him, but I had no faith myself and felt certain that nothing less than surgical aid could help him and that it would have to come soon. But he begged and pleaded, speaking just above a whisper, and at last knelt on the floor before me and taking my hands in his, placed them upon his throat entreating me to do something for him. Of course no normal human being could resist such a plea, so pray I did. Like a shock of lightning the power of God struck me and passed thru my body and out thru my arms into the young man. And this he felt like waves pass thru him and especially in his throat. It was so powerful that I almost fell to the floor and he shuddered and trembled. In less than fifteen seconds he jumped to his feet and began to praise God, his voice becoming more and more clear. He could turn his head in any direction and the tired, aching sensation had gone in an instant. It was his turn to be relieved from duty, so as the other driver came I walked with him to his home, which took no more than five minutes. The next morning there was no swelling, his throat was fully open and the physician at a loss to explain what had happened. The young man said, "I had lived on soup and gruel, sipped from a spoon for six days, and was terribly hungry. When I came home mother had roast beef and boiled potatoes, and I actually swallowed pieces as large as the end of my thumb." What had happened was self-evident.

CHAPTER XX

MIRACLES AND POWER—PART II

Most Powerful Manifestation There is probably no manifestation of the Holy Spirit in which the power of God is so manifested as in the casting out of demons. This may be why it is called a miracle as distinct from healing. There is a reason for this. In the prophesying, the speaking with tongues and interpreting, the Spirit uses the yielded body of a living person. In healings His operation is upon muscles, nerves, bones and fibers disordered by force or the result of disease. All of these require the exercise of some degree of power, but in each instance the person or matter is yielded or endeavoring to yield. In the casting out of demons the powerful resisting personality of the demon himself is encountered, who with might and main resists any interference from the man himself or the power of God. Only some one stronger than the demon can exercise any control over him and as some of the demons are very powerful the force required at times is enormous. Jesus hints at this in Matt. 12:28-29: "If I by the Spirit of God cast out demons, then is the kingdom of God come upon you. Or how can one enter into the house of the strong man, and spoil his goods, except he first bind the strong man? And then he will spoil his house."

Neither time nor space will allow any detailed study of demonology, but in order that the subject in hand be better understood some remarks concerning these individuals will be necessary. Just what is the origin of demons remains open to question. Some claim them to be fallen angels, or the devil's angels, or even a separate order distinct from either of these. That angels have fallen we know from the Scripture. "And the angels that kept not their own principality, but left their proper habitation, he hath kept in everlasting bonds under darkness unto the judgment of the great day." Jude 6. From the Word we have reason to believe that there are different orders of angels, each order differing from the other in power, glory, position, work and authority. Jude's writing leads one to believe that certain angels deliberately and willfully, and at the same time knowing what they were doing and what effect it would have upon the purpose of God's plans, left the position assigned to them and thereby rebelled against God's authority. For which reason He took away from them the glory, majesty and freedom usually associated with angels and placed them under bonds of darkness and unable to act except in darkness and under certain conditions favorable to themselves. Peter tells us, "God spared not angels when they sinned, but cast them down to hell, and committed them to pits of darkness, to be reserved unto judgment." 2 Peter 2:4.

Possible Demon Origin

Just what this sin was is hard to say. Some think that it was some form of unlawful intercourse with human beings. This is very possible as evidenced by the way demons deal with human beings to-day. It may have been both this and that of leaving their proper sphere of power in the heavenlies. Some object to the fallen angels being called demons, stating that the fallen angels are bound in chains and are in hell. But it happens that hell is not only a place, but a spiritual condition, and they are held in this condition of spiritual bondage and darkness until the judgment at the great white throne, when everyone whose name is not written in the book of life will be cast into the lake of fire.

Varying Demonic Power If the demons are fallen angels with corrupted wisdom and using their great knowledge for only evil, then we have some exceedingly powerful individuals to deal with and fight against. Paul says that we battle not against "flesh and blood, but against the principalities, against the powers, against the world-rulers of this darkness, against the spiritual hosts of wickedness in the heavenly places." Eph. 6:12. It is highly probable that those of the highest order seldom deal with human beings directly, but rather direct the demon activities in cities, states or even nations and have in turn above them the chief of the demons, Satan himself. These higher principalities apparently very seldom inhabit human beings except in certain rare cases. No doubt such self-styled prophets as Swedenborg, Mohammed, Joseph Smith and others claiming divine revelation, surely must have been visited and possessed by supernatural spiritual power, at least at times, if their narratives are true. It is quite certain that those of former days and to-day who are authors of these Christless, bloodless, religions both are and have been inspired by these anti-Christal principalities and powers that defy God.

It is the lesser ones that inhabit humans and even among these there are varying degrees of power, the removal of some only being accomplished thru special prayer and fasting. A witch doctor and medicine man, in one of the northern California Indian tribes, had some eight evil spirits at his command. By making covenant with one of the greater demonic powers who appeared to him at times in the form of a serpent and which he worshiped, he was given some seven evil spirits as attendants or servants. When called upon to perform witchcraft or healing, he conjured forth the smallest of these demons first and if this smallest one with his power was unable to do anything, each one in his order of increasing strength was called upon. If all seven were too weak to do anything the largest one was brought forth, and he most usually did what was asked. Reports come thru missionaries in Korea, China and the islands of the Pacific of the same thing. Some priests of the evil one are reported as having as many as two thousand evil spirits for their attendants as a reward for having covenanted to give their soul at death to some greater evil principality.

Demonic control over humans varies in power and may be roughly divided into two classes, demon obsession and demon possession. In demon obsession the person still possesses his mind and, in a greater or lesser measure, his will power, but feels himself tormented and compelled, at times, to do evil things against his will. This condition may be periodical or continuous. In the case of true demon possession the mind and will of the individual seems to be replaced in varying degrees by that of the demon. And this also may be periodical or continuous. Most commonly this form may be called insanity and may be very violent. Or it may be exceedingly passive, as in extreme melancholia.

Insanity Many to-day laugh at the idea of demon possession, claiming that all insanity is the result of mental or nervous disorders of various kinds. Some even go so far as to say that Jesus and His disciples were mistaken in dealing with the demoniacs of their time. Not all insanity is demon possession and without a doubt most insanity comes from and is the symptom of mental derangement, but this does not exclude the possibilities of demon presence or operation. As mentioned in another chapter, there is a natural resistance in every human being against any spiritual influence, good or bad, and as a consequence a person must willingly yield in order to come under the influence of the Holy Spirit. And the degree of this yieldedness determines the degree in which the Holy Spirit can take possession of the person. This natural resistance also operates against demonical influences and unless broken down affords an effective barrier against demon possession.

The demons, because of being bound and deprived of their once possessed freedom, are more or less unable to act except thru the agency of a human body and mind. Consequently they are continually seeking for some human habitation in which they can dwell and thru which they can operate. If man's natural resistance were not present they would take possession of every human being. No doubt they do live in many wild animals.

This natural resistance seems to lie in the will power and the stronger the will power the more effective it is, but this resistance can be broken down by two things: disease and sin. Any disease that will incapacitate the mind so as to render the will power weak, or destroy it, will open the way for the demons to take possession of that person, but this does not necessarily bring about that all weak-minded persons are demon possessed.

One young man in Minneapolis felt his mind slipping. Medical aid was of no avail. As the derangement increased he felt the presence of evil spirits, and a little later these appeared to him in visible forms like animals leaping at him. Still later they took possession of him and he became a raving maniac.

A young married woman thru sickness and worry became insane, with clearer moments in between, during which she could think and speak rationally and realize her ailment and condition. On being questioned some time later, while in a sanitarium and while perfectly rational and practically well, she said, "I could feel something come over me that actually made me do those things. I knew what I was doing and knew that it was wrong, but had no power to resist. One day I took my baby and rowed out into a lake and tried to drown myself and her. But on getting into the cool water the shock somewhat broke the spell over me. I am certain that this thing was the devil."

Sometimes these nervous and mental weaknesses will be inherited, producing insanity thru several generations. In dealing with insanity of this kind it is first necessary to remove the demon, and then pray for the healing of the mind. If the mind is not healed, the door is open for the demon who left, or for another still worse, to enter in, and the last condition becomes worse than the first.

Caused by Sin — The other thing which breaks down this resistance is sin. All sin in some way or another opens the way for the presence and

MIRACLES AND POWERS, PART II

operation of the devil, but some sins more than others. Sin produces an atmosphere in which the demons thrive and are more or less free to operate. In the same way, prayer and godliness produce an atmosphere in which the Spirit of God can operate, resulting in the salvation of souls, and revivals. Cursing and a violent temper when extreme produce flashes of temporary madness which may even bring murder, for which the individual is often later ashamed and sincerely repentant. The use of alcohol, narcotics and drugs may so weaken the will power that the person has no power of resistance, and many an addict becomes violently insane before death. The delirium tremens of the drunkard is nothing more or less than the power of hell revealing itself to the victim of an alcohol-soaked brain. The abuse of certain body functions will often produce the very same results and many are to-day in the insane asylum for this very reason.

When sin has opened the way for the power of hell, either in the form of demon obsession or possession, not only must the demon be removed but the sin must cease. If the person does not hate this sin and ask that its power over him be broken, it is of no use to pray. Either the demon will not go or else will come back again, taking others with him.

A young man, sane-minded most of the time, was tormented by demons that came upon him at night, causing him to cry out, disturbing others so that he could find no lodging place, and robbing him of sleep. This even came on during the daytime, so that he could not hold any position. He asked to be prayed for and this was done, bringing a few days' relief. But it returned. On being questioned he confessed to sin against his own body, but would not and could not give it up. The demon visitation became more and more frequent until at last he became a raving maniac and remained so.

Spiritists and others who deal with familiar spirits and demons parading under various names, often find it more or less difficult at first to yield sufficiently to produce contact with them. Later they find that these demons, so hard to woo at first, are equally hard to get rid of.

Spiritism After these evil spirits for a time have periodically made use of the faculties of a human body and mind, but not necessarily causing demon possession, they seem to think that this use is indisputably theirs and refuse to relinquish their hold. A young woman in San Francisco, more or less in ignorance of the nature of what was taking place, was made use of by a renegade preacher of the gospel who as a medium was dealing with evil spirits. Seven spirits with different names and personalities would under certain conditions, one at a time, enter into her, putting her into a state of trance. While in this state of trance the spirit then possessing her would speak and prophesy thru her. These trances were very weakening and becoming more frequent, her health was undermined and she desired that they cease. But the man had such a control over her that he compelled her to submit to these things against her will. Feeling herself helpless she appealed to some Christian people for aid.

She was told that these spirits were not those of dead humans as they represented themselves to be, but demons parading under these various names. At first she would not believe this, but being anxious for deliverance, asked for prayer and their removal. As prayer was being made, she cried out that one of the spirits, giving his name, was coming upon her, and quickly fell into a trance. Those praying then called this spirit by name, bound him by the blood of Christ and adjured him in the name of Jesus to come out, which after a short struggle he did. Each spirit acted the same way until all seven had been cast out. One calling himself "Red Hawk," professing to be that of an Indian chief, was very violent. The last one professed to be that of her dead mother, and this last she was loath to part with, but being at last persuaded that it was a demon like the others, she was willing and he also was cast out. She became happy and glad. In a few days she reported that these same spirits, which before had been on such friendly terms, now were appearing in the form of animals such as wolves, tigers, eagles, snakes, and so forth, and again demanding entrance. The one called "Red Hawk" appeared as a blood-thirsty hawk and was much more violent than the others. She asked for protection against these, and prayer was again offered and they left.

Epilepsy Epileptic fits are supposed by some medical men to be caused by some abdominal disarrangement, and this no doubt has something to do with it. Jesus treated this as demon possession, so it must be a combination of both, evidently the disorder opening the way for the demon to bring his power to play. A young man in Alaska, afflicted with epileptic fits, heard of some meetings to be held in Seattle and felt admonished to go there and be prayed for. On making his request he was given certain instructions, told to read the Bible and pray for a day, and then return. The next day came but he did not arrive. But on the second day following he did, with a bandage around his head and a severe scalp wound. He told that while on the way to the services on the evening appointed, he was taken with a fit and fell, striking his head on the curbstone. He was informed that it was a demon that caused his ailment and that he must unite with those praying in resisting it. As prayer was offered the demon was first bound and then cast out, the young man falling into a heap on the floor. He reported afterwards that as the demon was being bound he could feel something taking place within himself. He was met some years later and reported that no reoccurrence had taken place, altho at one time some six months later, the sensation that precedes an attack came upon him, but upon resisting it and praying, it left and never returned.

Violence Very few demons leave the human body without a terrible struggle. While holding services in a northern California town, a young married woman of some twenty-five years, felt convicted of sin and desired salvation. As the power of the Spirit increased a demon-influence threw her to the floor, writhing and screaming. Becoming very violent she pulled her hair, scratched her cheeks and attempted to gouge out her eyes. Physical force had to be used to hold her limbs and prevent serious injury. The demon was rebuked, bound and cast out, and in a few minutes she was quiet, normal and at peace with God.

The demons also at times will speak out as they did in the time of the Lord. In Sacramento as a service was commencing, a woman was heard weeping in the audience and on being questioned, was found to be of questionable character, but desiring salvation. As she knelt to pray, some evil power came upon her and she fell prostrate. Her voice became very coarse and heavy, like that of a man, and her countenance likewise. The evil power was commanded to leave her, but it answered back with a heavy bass voice, "I won't come out, I hate Jesus, I hate you, I won't serve Jesus, I won't come out." The people became frightened and some ran out. The demon was told to keep still and commanded in the name of Jesus to leave her, which after a short, sharp struggle he did. The woman's face changed and likewise her voice, and shortly she was happy in her new-found salvation.

Luke records the Master's encounter with a demoniac in this wise: "And when he was come forth upon the land, there met him a certain man out of the city, who had demons; and for a long time he had worn no clothes, and abode not in any house, but in the tombs. And when he saw Jesus, he cried out, and fell down before him, and with a loud voice said, What have I to do with thee, Jesus, thou Son of the Most High God? I beseech thee, torment me not. For he was commanding the unclean spirit to come out from the man. For oftentimes it had seized him: and he was kept under guard, and bound with chains and fetters; and breaking the bands asunder, he was driven of the demon into the deserts. And Jesus asked him, What is thy name? And he said, Legion; for many demons were entered into him." Luke 8:27-30.

This passage is self-explanatory and requires no interpretation. One remarkable feature is that these thousands of demons could combine and live in the man at the same time. A missionary from China reported dealing with a man that had eight hundred demons and on being delivered, they moved out some forty or fifty at a time, until all had left, the whole process covering a period of several hours.

While services were going on in a certain place a young woman at every mention of the blood would rise up and cry out in a peculiar manner. This took place several times until admonished to keep still, which she managed to do with difficulty. After the service two ministers spoke to her, asking if she knew what was wrong with her. She answered, "I know. I have demons, and I wish to be delivered." She was asked to withdraw from the crowd into a room used for prayer. In the presence of some others she knelt upon the floor, but felt herself unable to utter a sound. As the others prayed she fell prostrate, her limbs working and her body writhing like a snake. Her eyes became very peculiar, and her tongue long and pointed like that of a dog, and froth appeared at the mouth. Peculiar sounds issued from her throat in a coarse, unnatural voice. This increased in violence until she was barking and snapping like a dog, and those near moved back for fear of being bitten. Prayer seemed unavailing. One of the men in the name of Jesus adjured the demon to give his name and twice he answered, "Legion, Legion." The other man then, in the name of Jesus commanded this legion to leave. The struggle became exceedingly violent and suddenly ceased, giving the impression that the woman had died. For some moments she lay perfectly quiet and then she slowly sat up. Her eyes and face were perfectly natural and her voice pleasant. She praised God for deliverance and thanked those around her for what they had done.

Faith, In casting out demons, the one praying above
Courage all things needs great faith and great courage.
Needed Nothing but a powerful anointing of the
Spirit can produce this. If the one praying in any way fears, his efforts are useless. It is very necessary that the demon be bound before being removed, for when deprived of his abode he immediately seeks another. It has happened in many cases that the removed but unbound demon has immediately taken possession of another, and that often from among those present and looking on. Such as are afraid and fear are most susceptible to this, and it is very wise and even necessary to remove such people from the scene before anything is done. Anyone living a clean life and under the blood of Christ need have no fear, but others had better take care. The cast-out demon will sometimes follow the one from whom he had gone out or even the one who cast him out. Rebuking and resisting him in the name of Jesus will soon put an end to this.

Exceeding The anointing and power of the Spirit that
Powerful comes upon the one casting out the demon
Anointing is greater than in any other manifestation
of the Holy Spirit, and is also the most strength-sapping of them all. If the demon is powerful and resists, it usually leaves the one praying very weak and exhausted. In a very sinful city, a certain man, considered a good Christian, was seeking to be filled with the Spirit of God, and was mightily blessed from time to time. One evening it seemed as tho the

Spirit of God was actually filling him, but a queer atmosphere prevailed, and other things present caused some to doubt its genuineness. After a season of prayer it became evident that the power of the devil was operating instead of God. The pastor reported afterwards that he actually saw the demon beside the man. This he rebuked in the name of Jesus, but as he did so the virtue that is felt flowing out in praying for the sick, flowed out from his body like a tremendous current, and left him lying completely exhausted upon the floor. He had to be helped home, and slept nearly all of the twenty-four hours the first day, and eighteen the next, before he regained his strength. The question may be raised as to how the demon came to be present and work in such a way, imitating if possible the Spirit of God. The only explanation is that this was an exceedingly wicked city, full of vice and lust, with but a handful of praying people, and that thru this sin the atmosphere was made sufficiently congenial for the power of the devil to freely operate. After a few months of prayer and preaching many were converted and a revival broke out, and this presence of the devil was no longer felt.

Just as Jesus was to ascend unto His Father He said, "And these signs shall accompany them that believe: in My name shall they cast out demons." Mark 16:17. The name of Jesus has power because it sets in motion the power of God, and before Him all the forces of hell are helpless. When the name of Jesus is used no demon can operate. So when the name of Jesus is used for the healing of the sick and against demons, it must be the Spirit of God that works. We are often like the Apostle John, who wanted to limit the working of the power of God to his own little crowd, when he reported,

MIRACLES AND POWERS, PART II 233

"Teacher, we saw one casting out demons in thy name; and we forbade him, because he followed not us," to which Jesus replied, "Forbid him not: for there is no man who shall do a mighty work in My name, and be able quickly to speak evil of Me." Mark 9:38-39. This might be good advice to all of us.

As closing words of advice we might say: Have as little to do with demons as possible. Never attempt to cast them out without first possessing faith and courage. But remember, that in the name of Jesus all the powers of heaven lie at one's command, before which Satan must surely give way.

Method of Procedure   Anyone that is really saved has the authority to cast out demons. Those who have the baptism are best equipped. No two demons can be dealt with alike and the spirit of discernment is necessary in all cases. The most common method of procedure would be about as follows. If the person is sane and rational, if possible get him to unite his will with yours in resisting the demon. Get him to do some praying himself. If he is irrational, get his nearest relatives or friends to unite with you. Allow no unbeliever or person with lack of faith, whether saved or unsaved, to remain in the room or the near vicinity. Be sure to bind the demon in the name of Jesus before ever attempting to cast him out. Command him to come out in the name of Jesus. If talkative and violent command him in the name of Jesus to be silent and hold his peace. If very stubborn and hard to remove command him in the name of Jesus to give his demon name. Then addressing him in that name command him to come out and never return. If the one delivered is unsaved get him to immediately surrender to the Lord. If saved get him to consecrate his life to the Lord and keep it consecrated. Never beg or entreat a demon. It is useless. Never be afraid of him. Go at it determined to have the victory and insist upon it.

CHAPTER XXI

The Gift of Discernment

This gift is listed by Paul among the others, altho not given any prominence. 1 Cor. 12:10. To-day it is quite uncommon and rare altho its presence and operation would be of great blessing and save much trouble. In the early church it was far more prevalent than now, and for this there is a reason.

Needed by Early Church   When Christianity arrived on the scene it found the stage already occupied by many and powerful religions in which various spirits worked. It had to prove its own merits before obtaining a hearing or following. The religions of those days were in various degrees demonical in their origin and operation. Powerful spirits performed signs and wonders. The demon possessed priests and devotees were soothsayers and prophesied, and in so doing closely imitated the operations of the Holy Spirit. As far as the eyes and ears were concerned it was practically impossible to tell the difference. For this reason they of the early church needed something more than the ears and the eyes, and this was supplied by the Holy Spirit thru the gift of discernment.

There appears to be at least two forms under which this spiritual gift operates. In the one it seems as

Two Forms tho the mind of the person is used and certain tests are applied, and the other is where the Holy Spirit Himself speaks directly to the person.

The former seems to be what John has in mind when he says, "Beloved, believe not every spirit, but prove the spirits, whether they are of God; because many false prophets are gone out into the world." 1 John 4:1. The prophets prophesied by the spirit that dwelt in them and operated thru them. Thru these utterances the operating spirit revealed his identity. If the message magnified Christ it was God's Spirit speaking. But if it annulled and set at nought the Son of God then it was the spirit of antichrist or the devil as represented by one of his demons, that was doing the talking. In this case the person's ears, eyes and mind are of use. The spirit operating thru and dwelling in the man can be adjured in the name of Jesus and compelled to speak and tell of his attitude toward Jesus of Nazareth. It becomes very evident that any saved person with faith in God can apply these tests, so their use can hardly be called any special gift.

True Form The true gift of discernment appears to be a direct manifestation of the Holy Spirit thru some person, and which gift is more or less peculiar to that individual, such as the gift of healing or interpretation would be. In the operation of this gift the Spirit seems to pass on His information direct to the mind or spirit of the person, independent of any information received by the person thru any of the five senses.

The Spirit of God is in most excellent position to

THE GIFT OF DISCERNMENT

obtain whatever knowledge He desires. The Word says that He proceeds forth from the Father, so He must be full Deity. John. 15:26. And He searcheth all things, yea, the deep things of God. 1 Cor. 2:10. Evidently He knows all the thoughts and plans of God the Father. Being everywhere present He is acquainted with what the demonic powers are doing and planning, which information may be even hidden from the angels, unless revealed to them by God. He also knows men and before Him their thoughts are as an open book. This places at His disposal all the knowledge in the visible and invisible creation and nothing to the extreme limits of the universe is hidden from Him.

Thru experience and what others tell us we know a little of the past. By means of our five senses and knowledge gotten from others, we know a very small fraction of the present. Except as we may reason out the consequences of present conditions thru past experiences, and make some shrewd guesses, we know exceedingly little of the future. At best we are tremendously at a disadvantage because of our ignorance. Both angels and demons far excel us in wisdom and knowledge. And what may be going on among either of these classes is completely hidden from us. If, however, this wonderful all-knowing Holy Spirit is willing to impart to us some of His great immeasurable knowledge, then our limitation is greatly lessened and thru His help we are able to look into things hidden from ordinary mortals, and possibly from angels and demons, also.

Thru the gateway of our five senses all our information comes to us. Our eyes, ears, nose, taste and feelings send information to the brain and from

Our Five Senses this information the mind constructs impressions, thoughts and ideas. If any of these gateways are closed the information received is much lessened and the mind is much handicapped. If a person is blind, the ears and feeling must work all the harder and be more keen, and still the person misses much and must depend upon others who have eyes. Thus the mind is absolutely dependent upon the gateways for its operation. In the ordinary course of events the Lord will deal with us thru these senses and use these gateways. But at times when He wishes to pass on information incapable of being passed on thru any of these five senses He must speak to the mind or to our spirit directly. And this He does thru the Holy Spirit.

This same phenomenon takes place in spiritism. The medium will go into a state of trance thru the influence of some evil spirit, or demon, and then while in this condition, with all the senses subdued and inactive, the unclean spirit will speak directly to the mind or spirit of the medium, who on awakening will claim to have had a revelation. The Spirit of God can do the same thing, and when necessary does so. To Peter as a Jew, all Gentiles, according to the law, were unclean and no human being or angel ever could have served as a message-bearer to tell him to go into a Gentile home and there preach the Word. But while his five senses were set aside, when he was in a trance on the housetop, God brought him the message thru the Holy Spirit. Balaam while following Balak's leading, while his eyes were closed and lying on the ground, saw Israel's future history. Numbers 24. The prophet Ezekiel while

THE GIFT OF DISCERNMENT

sitting with the elders of Israel before him, fell into a trance and thru the Spirit saw wonderful things.

But the Holy Spirit can reveal things direct to the **mind and the spirit of** a person while awake. And when this revelation comes concerning other persons, spiritual conditions, demonic presence or the will of the Lord, it is called discernment of spirits. But this is not always limited to a waking condition as it may come while in a state of trance or even while asleep.

This operation is peculiar, to say the least, and most always is very puzzling to the person. It could hardly be anything but puzzling when the Spirit will give information that actually at times is directly contrary to what the ears hear and the eyes see, and the person is certain he knows to be the truth. But the Lord looks beyond the outside appearance and considers rather the condition of the heart; He does not judge after the appearing of the eyes and the hearing of the ears.

Independent of Senses   The operation of this gift seldom occurs except at such times as when a person's ordinary senses and mental faculties are incapable of detecting whatever falseness or devilishness may be afoot. And the singular thing is that most often in such cases the information passed on by the Spirit is directly contrary to the impressions received by the mind thru ordinary channels. This, of course, puts the person in the very difficult position of being between two fires; namely, that of his natural senses which ordinarily have served him well, and that of the inner voice of the Spirit which says something different.

In a small city, a pastor with his congregation was

richly blessed of the Lord. A man calling himself a preacher arrived and claimed himself sent of the Lord to take over the work. The pastor in a measure felt willing. But on praying the Holy Spirit said, "No, he is not the man. Beware of him." This admonition the pastor followed and obeyed as long as away from him, but on being in his presence this other man's bearing, language, fervor and persuasion completely disarmed him. So while away and while in prayer he felt that this other man was not sent of God, but while in his presence he doubted the leadings of the Spirit as he could see no wrong in the man. It did not take long, however, for things to come to a head which revealed the true state of affairs, and the newcomer left.

A pastor, on arriving home one evening, was told by his wife, that a stranger was in another room desiring to speak to him. The pastor's time was occupied, so that for some fifteen minutes he was unable to see, or speak to, this man. But long before he saw him he was strongly impressed that there was something wrong with the stranger and to have as little as possible to do with him. This newcomer claimed to be a missionary on the way to Africa. Shortly the Lord brought this scripture: "The prophets prophesy lies in My name; I sent them not, neither have I commanded them, neither spake I unto them: they prophesy unto you a lying vision, and divination, and a thing of nought, and the deceit of their own heart." Jer. 14:14. One of the members of the congregation had had a dream the night before this man arrived, and in it had been warned against a certain type of person having certain peculiar characteristics, and on seeing this man, instantly recognized him as the man in the dream. It shortly devel-

THE GIFT OF DISCERNMENT

oped that this man was a rank impostor traveling around the country collecting money for his professed missionary ventures which never materialized.

Thus in these two instances the operation of this gift of discernment detected the plans of the devil and by warning against coming danger prevented serious damage to the congregation. It is very probable that in practically every case where damage has come to assemblies thru the sneaking in of wolves in sheep's clothing, it could have been prevented if either someone had possessed the spirit of discernment or if the others had given heed to the warning given by the one possessing it.

Detects Sham Some persons carry a reputation along religious lines, being known as great men of God, when in reality they are not, but rather have managed by some means or other to build a halo around themselves which some people are not able to see thru. Not a few these days, like so many sheep, flock to the standards of men of this type and hang upon their every utterance as tho they were direct from God, often to their own damage and even destruction. A servant of the Lord from distant parts was invited to call upon one of these so-called great men for the purpose of making a profitable acquaintance. On entering this man's home he instantly felt in the Spirit that the degree of spirituality was far less than he expected to find. As the conversation drifted on he seemed lost in the Lord and hardly noticed what was being said. At the same time he seemed to feel as tho he could literally look into the very heart of this man and read his whole general make-up as tho it had been an open page. In this he saw that the man before him was of very mediocre caliber, less than what was expected in spirituality, and one that would not hesitate to shade a truth or even do another damage to win a point or further his own interests. Later years and further acquaintance bore this out to the letter.

This spirit of discernment is very effective and advantageous in determining the degrees of spirituality of a man in the pulpit. There are times when in a man's message or sermon no note of falseness can be detected. As far as the ears, eyes and mind are concerned he appears to be a true man of God. But in some peculiar and indescribable way those living close to the Lord can feel that something is wrong. How or why they cannot say, except that they feel it. Many an assembly has taken a pastor because of his first good impressions, only to find later that they had something on their hands that they badly wanted to get rid of. The Holy Spirit thru the operation of the gift of discernment could have prevented this.

Needed by Pastors The possession of this gift is of great advantage and help to evangelists or religious public speakers. The most effective public speaker is the one who can supply just what is suited to the audience then present. Material prepared days in advance is good, but unless the speaker has some way of knowing just who will be there and in what spirit they will come, it does not always fit the occasion. But such knowledge beforehand is humanly impossible. However, the Spirit of God, who searches all things and knows the future, can supply this very information. A man

THE GIFT OF DISCERNMENT

walking close to the Lord may be able thru the Spirit to sense a coming service days in advance.

Possibly the best result in discerning the spirit of a gathering is produced when it comes just as the audience gathers and the service starts. Some of those men of God whose message is almost invariably honored by the power of God do but little outlining or preparing of the message beforehand, aside from the reading of the Word and considerable praying. They prefer to "read" or "feel" their audience and then supply its needs. Each audience has a spirit of its own and no two audiences are alike even tho consisting of the same people. So material once used to advantage and blessing does not always produce the same results the second time. But being in position to feel just what the gathering then present needs, and also possessing sufficient biblical and other knowledge for the Holy Spirit to draw upon, that man can give out true meat in due season and be wonderfully used of the Lord.

A certain man much used of the Lord in revival work will often enter the place of meeting without knowing what to speak on for the evening. He prefers to arrive a little early and then sit undisturbed and "feel" his audience. After some minutes he discerns the spirit of the gathering and almost as quickly the Holy Spirit will give the scripture that becomes the message for the evening. Almost without exception this produces results and brings the response, "That is just what was needed."

Praying for Sick

In praying for the sick this gift also operates to advantage. Spiritually, sickness may be roughly classed under three heads: that caused by disobedience against the common laws of nature and decent living; that sent by the Lord as a means of ultimate blessing, such as Job and his boils; and that caused primarily by the devil, such as the woman who had been bound by the devil for eighteen years, but who was healed by Jesus. If disease is caused by incorrect living, it is not only necessary to pray for the removal of the disease, but also to correct the manner of living, as otherwise it will quickly come back. Plain medical knowledge or even everyday common sense can supply this information, so no special discernment is needed. But if the Lord has an object in view in allowing disease to rest, the best possible move is to find what that object is and as far as possible bring it to pass. Prayer and waiting on the Lord will soon make this clear. The Lord had an object in view in allowing the devil to torment Job with a crop of boils. No matter how much someone would have prayed and petitioned heaven, they would have remained and did remain until their work was done. The one praying for the sick needs the discernment in order to detect conditions like this, and a more general possession of this gift would prevent a lot of promiscuous praying for the sick, which in too many cases has brought damage rather than glory to the Lord's cause.

This discernment becomes very pronounced at times. A man was asked to call upon and pray for an old woman seriously ill and for three months bedridden and helpless with an abdominal cancer. On entering the home he instantly felt a conviction that the woman would be healed. She later reported that the instant he entered the house she felt the same assurance. The day after being prayed for she was out walking in the

THE GIFT OF DISCERNMENT

garden. In another case this same man was asked by a mother to call and pray for a daughter sick with a long-standing ailment. Some twenty-four hours before going and while in prayer he felt a powerful impression that the Lord's presence would be very pronounced. And such it was to the healing of two members of the family instead of one, the salvation of another present and the restoration of still another, and a general blessing upon the whole household, which had lasting results.

Detects Demon Presence   If the presence of a demon is the instigator of the sickness and his presence is not detected, the prayer will produce but little results. Some of these demons are dormant or quiet and manifest themselves in no way capable of detection. But thru God's Spirit their presence becomes known and they can be cast out.

Senses Spiritual Atmosphere   Not only is this gift of benefit in discerning the spirit operating in a church or a gathering, but also makes known the religious atmosphere of a home. A home in which much prayer is offered and where holiness abides becomes filled with the presence of God. If strife and wrangling is common a spirit of uneasiness fills the air. If false doctrines and demon religions, such as Spiritism, Christian Science, Hindu cults and others, without the blood or deity of Christ, are believed in and practiced, they produce a general demonic atmosphere and also an atmosphere of their own. These can become so pronounced as to be noticed by unsaved persons. A keen spirit of discernment will detect this as soon as the house is entered or after a few minutes of conversation, not so much by what is heard or seen but by what is felt. Sleeping in such a home may become a succession of nightmares and demon visitations. Different cities have different spiritual atmospheres. One with many praying inhabitants will feel pure and comparatively clean. Another full of vice, sin and moral degradation, has its atmosphere actually well populated with demon power, making it very difficult for its people to pray or have faith, and almost impossible to preach the gospel with any liberty, or for the Holy Spirit to work in bringing conviction of sin unto salvation. In cities where Christless, bloodless cults dominate this becomes very pronounced. Some persons have this gift of discernment so developed that they can sense these things on passing thru a city on the train, or on alighting at the station platform, or in a few minutes' walk thru its streets. In all heathen lands this demonic atmosphere is so strong that no special gift is needed to discern it. At times this pressure becomes terrific and more so during such times as when the evil spirits are especially worshiped.

The gift of discernment differs from most of the other gifts of the Spirit in that it is direct to the individual and has no external manifestation. It also varies with each individual and also in the individual himself. And almost no two operations of the gift are alike. This combines to make this gift very difficult to describe and almost impossible to lay down any hard and fast rules for.

Is Not Own Thoughts   Many interpret the workings of their own mind to be the leadings of the Holy Spirit and consequently consider themselves as possessing the gift of discernment when it

THE GIFT OF DISCERNMENT 247

is only their own head working overtime. A person needs to be very careful about using the expression, "The Lord showed me." The Holy Spirit does not tell lies or reveal things that are not true. A woman seeking for more of the Lord did not seem to get anywhere. Another woman made her the subject of special prayer and shortly came back with a "revelation from the Lord," saying that she never would receive anything until she removed her false hair. The seeking one told the one with the revelation to remove it, and lo and behold! she had no false hair. So God was not at the bottom of that revelation, but rather she was the victim of her own over-zealous ideas.

Not to be Peddled — Others make the great mistake of promiscuously peddling information imparted by the Holy Spirit. This soon quenches the gift and many have lost it for this reason. Most of the Spirit's revelations are of a private nature, and are given for the purpose of guiding the person himself, or for use so as to make him of help to others. By the use of this gift one knows how to pray and what to pray for, what to preach and how to act and order one's self toward others, what dangers to guard against and how, but not in order to proclaim from the housetops what a wonderful person he is because of what the Lord has revealed.

Altho all persons possess some degree of discernment, it becomes more pronounced when the baptism of the Spirit occurs. But not all those baptized, altho possessing some of it, have the full gift.

As with many of the other gifts and manifestations of the Spirit, some naturally lend themselves to its operations much more readily than others, and besides this the Holy Spirit divideth to each one severally as He will. Like some of the others, it can be obtained thru prayer, but not if the motives are selfish. The early church needed it badly, but to-day's conditions are equally so in need of its operations. Much of this modern theology and its devilish teachings and many of these smooth, slick sons of the devil in many pulpits could have been kept out if this gift had been in operation. Let us pray for its more general return to the church.

Needed To-day

CHAPTER XXII

Order in the Assembly

This chapter consists more or less of gleanings and left-overs from the others. It therefore will not be as orderly and consecutive in thought as it might be. In it various points that were hardly touched upon, or just hinted at, are dwelt upon more fully. Much more can be said than is presented here and it would be needful too. But enough can be found in it to be of blessing to anyone that is willing to learn. There are those who profess to know it all and never will learn, no matter how much is said.

In nearly every instance that the power of God has been poured out and the Holy Spirit has supernaturally manifested Himself, certain untimely, unseemly, and even disgusting manifestations and actions have taken place which have done much to harm and discredit the work as a whole. Because of their effect in discrediting the real work of the Spirit they very evidently do not have their origin in God, for the Spirit of God is not the author of confusion and does not operate to tear down what He is Himself endeavoring to build up. This leaves for our consideration only two agents that possibly can be the cause—plain everyday flesh and the power of the devil.

One of the most common forms in which the flesh likes to parade is in the misuse of the gifts and manifestations of the Spirit. This misuse is not limited to our time only, as it was present in apostolic days and Paul found it rampant in the Corinthian church. The burden of his theme in the twelfth, thirteenth and fourteenth chapters of the First Epistle to the Corinthians is the question of order in the assembly, and it is this misuse of the gifts that he is trying to correct. The underlying cause of this misuse is mostly ignorance and selfishness.

All the manifestations of the Holy Spirit are accompanied by a greater or less feeling of the presence of the power of God and an ecstasy upon the one so exercised. Many persons are so carnal that they wish to have these feelings at all times and literally live in them. Some go so far as to think that they have lost out unless these are continually present. These seekers for feeling of course have a preference for those manifestations which bring the most of it, such as speaking with tongues, interpretations, and singing and praise in the Spirit. Naturally, those desiring these spiritual sensations in the flesh seek for and use these particular gifts and manifestations in season and out of season. With many, everything is weighed on a basis of feelings, and a message or meeting is judged by the amount of sensation it produces while it is in progress. Others seem to so chase feelings that their main purpose in going to a service or gathering is to obtain them. Some are such slaves to this that they cannot stay at home for one evening, even neglecting their families and home life.

But seeking for feeling is not always limited to the audience—it even sometimes gets into the pulpit. Some pastors cannot preach until the gathering has reached a certain pitch of enthusiasm and will use almost any method to produce this. But the over-emphasizing of feelings and stirring up the enthusiasm will often go so far as to crowd the preaching of the Word out of its proper place. The presence of the power of God upon a service can always be enjoyably felt both by the saved and unsaved, and without it the Word is dead, lifeless and brings no results. So let us thank God for these feelings for they are good and have their proper place, but at their best they are but dessert rather than the solid meat of our soul-food. Dessert for a steady diet does not produce much growth or development. Many a service, or even series of meetings, which has produced a great riot of feeling has left the hearers nothing to take home but a memory of much and many spiritual sensations. This does not develop rooted and grounded saints, and later affords little or no protection against temptation, sin and the devil. But the sensible preaching of the Word under the anointing of the Spirit does, for He anoints the mind of the speaker and the understanding of those who hear, and the knowledge thus gained is remembered, and being stored away in the heart, becomes a lamp unto the feet and a guide unto the pathway.

Many in their incessant striving for sensations endeavor to bring about the operation of their various feeling-accompanying gifts as often as possible. Many are so shallow as to think that their salvation depends upon the presence of these things at all times, and therefore feel bound to do something to keep them operating continuously. There is nothing said in the Scriptures about how we shall act in our private devotions, but nevertheless, common sense can even here be used. However, when the continuous play of these gifts takes place in the presence of others, and especially during the general gatherings, it conflicts with the Word of God, for Paul's advice is that all things shall be done unto edifying, decently and in order. 1 Cor. 14:40. But some are so stupid, self-willed and ignorant, and so steeped in selfishness that they cannot consider anyone but themselves, and in satisfying their desire for feelings and sensations, do not hesitate to trample and ignore the rights and privileges of others. Very often the actions of people of this kind keep many sensible and hungry souls from seeking the deeper things of salvation. These hungry ones can see that these things are unscriptural. They are at a loss to understand how they can be called of the Holy Spirit, and so become confused and discouraged.

But the misuse of the gifts is not caused by feeling-seeking and selfishness alone. An equally great producer of confusion is the lack of discerning as to when, or how, to use them. Because of this ignorance and lack of discernment many conscientiously believe that every visitation of the power of God upon them is for the purpose of bringing about the operation of their peculiar and personal gift. Herein they make a great mistake. They fail to realize that the Spirit of God does not always wish to manifest Himself thru some gift, and may have some altogether different reason or purpose for His presence. This error is common. It is noticeable that when a wave of God's presence sweeps over a gathering of baptized saints, almost invariably a considerable number of them will interpret this as the time to give way to any leading or desire that may come along. Some will speak with tongues, others praise or sing, and still others just shout and yell at the top of their voices, all of which co-mingles to produce what sounds to an outsider like utter confusion and bedlam. The scriptural order under such conditions, it seems, would be that when the Spirit moves upon a gathering to bring praise, then let those praise upon whom the Spirit of praise rests and let the others keep silent. Sometimes the Holy Spirit will use several in a gathering to praise by singing in the Spirit, which manifestation, when without flesh adjuncts, is very edifying both to those exercised and to those who hear. Others feeling the presence of the Lord will cut loose with promiscuous tongues, speaking, yelling and shouting, which utterly ruin the effects of the melody and hinder the Spirit from bringing to the gathering the blessing that He intended to bring thru that song or singing. This singing in the Spirit is heavenly and some years back when it was much more prevalent than now, there were those especially used in this manifestation, but flesh seems to have spoiled much of it. If the saints as a whole had more discernment and could better control themselves, their gifts, and their flesh, the Holy Spirit could bring forth many wonderful things, but as things are now He is hindered and actually prevented from doing so by the very people that He wishes to use.

Then at other times, when a real spirit of intercession and a burden of prayer settles down upon a gathering, real results might be accomplished if this were allowed to run its course. Here again will come confusion. Others, not discerning that it is prayer that the Spirit desires, will begin to sing, or to shout, or to praise, or do something else completely out of order for the time being, breaking the atmosphere of prayer and driving away the spirit of intercession.

In one large evangelistic campaign the morning hours were used for prayer exclusively. First came some minutes of waiting upon the Lord to find the Spirit's leading so as to know what to pray for. Following this the general prayer set in and lasted as long as the spirit of intercession rested, which often was several hours. All other manifestations were hushed. Anyone speaking in tongues or singing in the Spirit and not entering into the spirit of the meeting, was told to keep silent. Many wondered at the scripturalness of such proceedings, but God wonderfully honored it by a real outpouring of His presence to the salvation, healing and baptism of many.

Some are under the impression that the gifts of the Spirit are given in order to be purposely displayed. A certain assembly was wild with fanatical manifestations, such as unrestrained speaking with tongues, shoutings, groans, handclapping, ridiculous jerkings of the body and the limbs, and peculiar twistings of the head. After a few weeks of the Word of God and some carefully given advice most of this ceased. Some objected strenuously to any attempt to put a stop to it, saying that it would be fraught with much danger on account of "quenching the Spirit." But instead, the Spirit honored it and real messages in tongues and interpretations came forth and also times of intercession and prayer. Several thanked God for the change in the order of things. One woman said, "I am glad that you came and that you told us these things. I used to think that when the power of the Spirit came on me and the rest of us in the meetings we were to do everything we could to show those looking on just what the Spirit could do, and as a result made a fool out of myself. Now my eyes are open and I get deeper and greater blessings than ever before."

When the true speaking in tongues, interpretation and prophecy in the Spirit come forth in their proper place, the effects are good and very edifying and uplifting. This is really the main purpose in the Spirit's bringing them. If, however, they are not rightly used, the intended blessing and edification are of course lost, but, worst of all, a spirit of confusion and sense of disorder sets in, which breaks the natural spiritual progress of the service. The proper spiritual order is for one to give the message in the tongue and for another, or the speaker himself, to interpret. When the Holy Spirit is about to give such a message and to interpret, a peculiar presence of the Spirit comes which all baptized saints can more or less feel, and especially those that are ordinarily used in the operation of this gift. When this is felt it often happens that those who possess the gift are not able to discern whether it is themselves or some other that the Spirit wishes to speak thru and often get up and speak out of time. Sometimes this may be caused by just selfishness and a desire to be seen and heard, or it may be a desire to have the wonderful blessing that being so exercised brings. But generally the persons are honest and sincerely desire to serve the Lord, but possess too much zeal and too little knowledge. Because of lacking the necessary wisdom they run ahead of the Lord and the order of the Spirit.

It happened in a service that as the preacher was speaking he gave a message in tongues which was interpreted. This was followed by another message in tongues given by one sitting by, which also was interpreted. Just as this last interpretation came to an end, suddenly some five persons jumped to their feet at once and all at the same time gave a different message in tongues. This, of course, spoiled the effect of the former messages, brought confusion and almost broke the spirit of the whole service. One or two of these possibly were seeking for a little notoriety, but the others simply without waiting sufficiently on the Lord undertook to exercise their gift out of season. When they had sat down the one who had given the second message in the tongue gave another, which in turn was interpreted. Such instances happen again and again, but could be prevented and set in order thru a little wise advice or asking the Lord for wisdom.

But probably greater confusion results when two or more try to interpret the same message. Here the same running ahead of the Spirit enters in, but with it comes the taking of one's own thoughts as the voice of the Spirit. When the power to interpret comes upon a person it usually strikes like a flash of fire and is much more violent and powerful than the anointing to speak in tongues. As the time to interpret approaches, all those possessing the gift feel some of the presence of the Spirit. But many make the mistake of not waiting until the true anointing arrives which brings the words to be said. Consequently they get up without it and have nothing but the thoughts of their own mind to give out, which of course are flat and empty and easily discerned as such by the hearers.

When two different interpretations come for the same message in tongues something is radically wrong somewhere. The Spirit of God surely does not give each a different interpretation. Then He would be the author

ORDER IN THE ASSEMBLY

of confusion and almost a liar, which of course cannot be. So one must have been right and the other wrong; one was in the Spirit and the other in the flesh. If three or four each give a different interpretation to the same message, then the condition is still worse. The truth probably is that one received the real message and the others were brain-manufactured and given in the strength of the flesh. Sometimes it happens when the plural interpretations are thus given that none of them are right. When the real interpretation comes it is easily recognized. If the first interpretation is in the flesh the others who interpret can feel it, and then in trying to right the wrong run ahead of the Spirit and give another in the flesh, making conditions worse instead of better. By the time a few more have added some more in the flesh to it, it becomes a fine mess. The secret in powerful interpretation lies in holding still and waiting upon the Lord until the real anointing comes, and if an assembly is taught to practice this there usually is no confusion and a beautiful order in the Spirit prevails, edifying its members and bringing respect from the outsiders.

One individual who was used to interpret, was told by some that he was trying to show off and his message was not of the Lord. Being honest he felt hurt and asked the Lord to take it away if it was not from Him. So at the next service he determined not to say anything no matter what happened. As he was quietly speaking to another, some one, a stranger, gave a message in tongues, to which he paid no attention. As the other finished, suddenly and without warning the power of the Spirit came powerfully upon him like a flash of fire, and almost against his will a very strong and powerful message came forth. This proved to him that it was of the Lord, and that he had not caused it by expecting it or by his own trying to urge it on.

Others misuse their gifts thru overvaluing them and considering them of more importance than the preached Word. The preaching of the Word under the anointing of the Spirit is the most important manifestation of the power of God. At a service two persons, each much used in giving messages in tongues and interpreting, were present. As the power of God began to come upon the meeting just before the preaching, they each gave several messages that were good, and had it stopped there all would have been well, but it did not. Instead it went on for a considerable length of time until each had spoken some eight or ten times, lasting all of half an hour. Long before they were thru the people became restless and uneasy. The spirit of the meeting was broken and the whole performance became flat, empty and almost nauseating. It broke the anointing for the preaching and considerable time had to be spent in singing and praying to clear the atmosphere.

Misuse of the gifts, thru seeking feelings and thru ignorance causes confusion enough. But when just everyday flesh is mingled with the manifestations of the Spirit the condition is worse. All true manifestations of the Spirit are very beautiful. Real clear-cut, clean messages in tongues, interpretations or prophecies are very uplifting and bring great blessing to any honest hearer. For any manifestation to come forth in purity the person must be so yielded that the flesh does not interfere. But not all have reached this place, with the result that their manifestations are part flesh and part Spirit. Many, for instance, will start interpreting in the Spirit and as the anointing ceases, being unable to check the flow of their own thoughts, these will crowd in. The last portion of the message will not be from the Lord but simply the thoughts of their own mind. Others will have certain pet phrases and utterances that they will use in every interpretation. Thus one person starts every message with "My people, my people" whether the interpretation is for saints or sinners. God never calls the unsaved His people, so that a part of the message, at least a portion of the time, is self-manufactured. Still others not knowing how to let the power of the Spirit "soak in," that is, work inwardly, will let it run loose in their flesh, producing all manner of shakings and motions that attract attention from the message to the one speaking. The purpose of the operation of any gift is to get the Word into the hearts of the hearers, and anything that hinders such can hardly be said to be caused by the Lord.

There are those who never have received any clear or definite gifts but have instead some peculiar manifestation which is almost impossible to catalogue. Some when the power of the Spirit comes upon them scream, others yell, still others do both, accompanied by some queer motions of arms, legs, body or head. Still others will have a spasm of shaking that looks like the ague.

Where some of these unseemly things come from is a puzzle and a question. Probably most of them originated while the baptism was being received. While the Spirit of God is brooding over a person, and as He is preparing the body for His moving in, He operates upon every part of the body until it is completely yielded to Him. This the flesh resists, causing various tremblings and shakings. But when the body is fully yielded and as the Spirit moves in, all this ceases and nothing but the presence and power of God is felt and noticed. However, after the baptism many associate these shakings in the flesh with the power of God, and every time they feel the power of God upon them they expect and encourage a corresponding something in the flesh which, of course, under these conditions they soon get. The natural run of events is for these things to wear off after a time, but with some who are more carnal than spiritual, these are so sought for and encouraged that they get worse instead of better. Once the habit is well intrenched it is very difficult to break.

There are those who have so long associated flesh and Spirit that they cannot tell them apart. If anyone mentions the need of order or tries to discourage this parading of the flesh, instantly a cry is raised about "putting your hand on the work of the Lord." And they are sincere about it, too, and will staunchly defend what they think is right. Not only that, but because of their sincerity and honesty of heart, God will bless them, not because they are right, but rather in spite of their being wrong. The fact that the Lord blesses a person is no sign that He approves all that he does. God looks to the spirit in which a thing is done rather than to its results.

For several reasons these flesh manifestations are harmful. First of all, they produce a shallowness in those possessing them in that they actually hinder and prevent the Holy Spirit from developing them as He wishes. Any attempt on His part to give them an edifying gift or bring them deeper into Christ never gets any further than their flesh. Many who have earnestly sought for real gifts in the Spirit would have long ago received, but when the anointing of the Spirit came upon them to bestow these gifts, they wasted it all in useless operations in their flesh. These flesh manifestations are at their best but evidences of Christian infancy or early childhood. Paul says that when he was a child, he spoke as a child, felt as a child, and thought as a child, but that after he had become a man, he put childish things aside. 1 Cor. 13:11.

They are also harmful in that they produce an atmosphere of spiritual carnality and childishness which affects all that come in contact with it. Persons coming to a knowledge of the baptism where there is decency and order become decent and orderly, while those coming to the truth of these things where the flesh is rampant get under the impression that such is the way the Spirit works and become fanatical. They then in turn spread this wherever they go, so that some assemblies are creating a fanatical influence for miles around and are very instrumental in propagating this atmosphere over considerable territory.

But the greatest harm is done toward the many thousands of hungry souls that desire more of God, but who are kept away because of these things. Because of their knowledge of the Word of God they know that these things are not scriptural, and act and speak accordingly. For this reason they are accused of being proud and told to humble themselves and suffer the reproach. When God gives a person an average amount of common sense and decency, He expects him to use it, and it is criminal to so prostitute one's intelligence as to allow oneself to be compelled to call certain things of the Lord, that an ordinary knowledge of the Word and everyday "horse sense" show are not. If the Spirit of God makes a person hunger and thirst for Himself, will He then also put it upon another to do some things that drive the hungry one away from the very thing the Holy Spirit has made him seek for? And yet these flesh manifestations are doing that very thing.

Many claim that they cannot control themselves and that the Spirit compels them to do these things. The Spirit does not compel anyone, for "He shall guide you into all the truth." John 16:13. Paul says that "the spirits of the prophets are subject to the prophets." 1 Cor. 14:32. Any manifestation of the Spirit can be controlled. The very fact that they are so difficult to handle, quite definitely evidences that their origin is in the flesh. There is probably no manifestation of the Spirit as hard to quench as a powerful anointing to preach the Word. But even that can be quenched, and likewise a message in tongues and an interpretation. Cannot then a little flesh be quieted down, if necessary?

A speaker standing before a strange and critical but friendly audience, felt the power of the Spirit come so mightily upon him that it burned thru his flesh and bones like molten fire. If he had been like some he would have jumped, screamed, yelled, or spoken a torrent of words in an unknown tongue. But realizing that any or all of these would have instantly made the whole audience antagonistic and spoiled the effect of his message, he asked the Lord to let this anointing not stop in his flesh but become effective in giving out the Word. And this it did.

The flesh manifestations at times can do great harm. At the close of a service in a revival campaign in which souls were saved from night to night, a very powerful spirit of conviction came. As the time for the decision arrived and many were powerfully stirred, a woman arose and screamed several times at the top of her voice. Instantly the spirit of conviction was broken and the whole service went flat. She claimed to be led by the Spirit and said that the power of the Spirit was upon her. Can it be possible that the Holy Spirit first anointed the preacher so that a whole audience was under conviction, and then anointed her to scream so that all this conviction was lost? Then He would be the author of confusion and His house divided against itself. No doubt the power of God was upon her, but she added the flesh part herself.

In places where flesh is encouraged rather than discouraged some queer things happen. A woman arose to testify, apparently under the power of the Spirit. Everything went well until she began to scream, "It is Jesus! It is Jesus!" She bent over and jumped up and down, and falling on the floor rolled around a few times, her clothing becoming disarranged, and finally came to rest prostrate with her head under a bench. Does the Holy Spirit cause things to happen that border on the obscene and compel people to hide their faces for shame? In the same audience a man picked up an eighteen-year-old young woman and carried her around like an infant, while another poked his fist thru a window. Still another, ignorant of any musical knowledge, but claiming to be led by the Spirit, sat down at the piano and pounded away, producing a mess of ear-jarring discords. These performances violated the sense of decency and propriety in most of those present, but when the pastor arose and vehemently proclaimed that these things were of the Holy Spirit many of his best members went out and permanently remained away.

A well built and beautiful young woman of some seventeen years had a habit of jerking her whole body, twisting her spine and throwing her head in a very peculiar way, and at the same time uttering some queer sounds that were partly screams and partly words. This was explained as a special anointing of the Spirit, which when resting upon any one, would result in the healing of the sick if touched. Naturally this one, and others so exercised, were looked upon as something great and this manifestation became very desirable, and still others sought it. Later it was discovered that some of these most blessed in this manner were doing things that caused a questioning of their Christian experience.

Real dancing in the Spirit is beautiful and uplifting to the one so exercised and to those who behold. But when those dancing smash furniture, strike others so that the blood flows, fall and almost break their necks, neglect prayer and lose the victory in their lives, then it has gone too far. What has begun in the Spirit has ended in the flesh. Are the manifestations of the Spirit such as to bring vulgar hilarity and loud guffaws from questionable characters from the streets, and produce more entertainment for them than if they had gone to the theater?

Remember this, the Spirit of God is holy like the Father from whom He proceeds. He is decent, clean, and pure, and makes people such. He does not crow like a rooster, tear off a woman's clothing, do bodily damage to those possessing Him or to others; He does not act unseemly, bark like a dog, spit and hiss like a snake, scream or hoot like an owl, or compel a person

ORDER IN THE ASSEMBLY

to act like one insane. Such are the doings of the flesh, and possibly of the devil.

How to handle these things is a difficult question to solve. Some follow the line of least resistance and let everything go. This, of course, gives a degree of liberty that the Spirit of God can operate in, but it also gives great liberty to the flesh, and of this liberty the flesh soon makes a license. Flesh turned loose does more damage than the Spirit can counteract. The other alternative is to quench the flesh completely and this naturally produces the sought-for order, but too much restraint causes a fear and bondage which prevent the Spirit Himself from working, and the whole thing becomes as dead as a cemetery. Others assume a middle course, saying that it is better to put up with a little wild fire in order to have the real fire, than not to have any fire at all. Possibly the safest way is to limit as far as possible all manifestations to those recorded in the Scripture, and to a few others clearly known to be of the Lord. All others we have a right to question or even firmly suppress, if necessary. Both the pastor and the evangelist need to know the Word along these lines and to practice it, lest they set a flesh example for the others. Then knowing it, they also need to have wisdom, and to be diplomatic and systematic with such as are in error. At the same time they need to give correct teaching and discourage unseemly and harmful things.

Flesh causes confusion enough, but the power of the devil is even worse. At times and in places where too great a liberty is given, and there is no attempt to maintain order, even demons take the liberty to perform thru human bodies. Let it here be said that great care need be exercised in attributing any manifestation to the devil until certain that it is such, for great damage may result to the individual so doing. All sin against the Father and the Son can be forgiven; but sin against the Holy Spirit is not forgiven, neither in this age, nor in the one to come. Any one willfully and knowingly attributing to the devil any act or power of the Holy Spirit becomes guilty of this. Demon operation is in some ways less common and in others more common than is supposed. Most of the things attributed to demon operation are nothing but unbridled flesh, possibly urged on by the devil. . But it does happen that demons do manifest at times, and that these manifestations are taken by some as of the Holy Spirit.

In a certain place where much speaking in tongues took place, one individual, whose life was not above reproach, spoke for a considerable length of time in an unknown language. Later another reported that he knew this language and that what the man had uttered was violent oaths. At another time when a man spoke in tongues another reported that he had uttered some of the vilest oaths in the Japanese language.

Flesh manifestations are usually ridiculous and possibly at the most disgusting. Demon operations are horrible and give the hearers a feeling of being in the presence of something awful, terrible and unclean. In an assembly where flesh and disorder were rampant, a certain woman seeking for the baptism of the Spirit, when praying, would go thru some horrible and awful contortions and groans and coarse utterances, which drove all spirit of prayer from the others. She was dealt with, but said that she could not help it and that the "Spirit compelled her." One evening as she was

ORDER IN THE ASSEMBLY

attempting to admonish another, she became very violent and loud in her utterances and shortly fell on the floor, screaming and kicking. Several looked on puzzled, but others rebuked the unclean spirit and told him to keep silent. For this they were severely criticized by some who said that they had rebuked the Spirit of the Lord. A day or two later the woman privately confessed to having intercourse with unclean spirits and asked for advice and deliverance.

A son of a minister of the gospel had for years shown himself very unresponsive toward the Word of God. During a revival campaign he seemed affected, and at the last service was powerfully under conviction. On speaking to him the evangelist placed his hand upon the young man's shoulder, and as he did so, the young man fell in a heap on the floor. He began to pray himself, but shortly became very violent, clawed the carpet, uttered coarse, harsh sounds, and kicked considerable plaster from the wall. The unclean spirit was rebuked and cast out and the boy became quiet, and shortly after arose professing salvation. He said that as the evangelist touched him he felt as tho a flash of fire had gone thru his whole body, and later he became unconscious and knew nothing of what had taken place. Other Christians looking on were surprised that the thing had been rebuked, thinking that the whole performance was of the Lord.

Much of the confusion lies at the door of the leaders of the assemblies and to some extent the evangelists. An old saying is, "Like priest, like people," and such is exceedingly true in this case. If the pastor or leader leans toward fanaticism, and seems to encourage questionable things, it does not take long for the flesh to take full advantage of the liberty given. If the leader is wise and discourages loose things, wild fire finds that it is not wanted and soon leaves. God, thru the old prophet cried, "My people are destroyed for lack of knowledge," and that is what is happening now. If people would use the Word as a basis of conduct, rather than their own or some others' experience, there would be far less disorder. But this spirit of individualism which so dominates both pastors and laymen prevents many from being taught, or receiving advice. So that it almost looks as tho some of the older ones were beyond aid, and the only hope is for the Lord to raise up some level heads from among the younger generation and this process is now going on.

Order in the assembly is necessary for personal and congregational growth and development. The average person has more common sense than he usually is credited with. He can easily tell the difference between the real and the unreal. When there is no order in the assembly many are attracted by the noise and the commotion, but on seeing the unscriptural and haphazard way that things are run, they soon become disgusted and leave. When scriptural order prevails the orderliness tends to hold those that come, and to act as a drawing card for such as prefer order. The fanatical assembly attracts fanatics and spreads fanaticism far and wide. The orderly assembly attracts order-loving people and spreads a wholesome stabilizing effect over much territory.

What seems to be the scriptural order for a general service? That might be briefly answered by saying that the general service should be so ordered as to be attractive to the outsider and the sinner and so conduct-

ORDER IN THE ASSEMBLY

ed that he will be influenced by the power of God present to turn to the Lord. Anything in a service that tends to drive away an honest, seeking soul should be eliminated and discouraged. Too much praying—too much preaching—too much singing—too much manifestation and too much of anything, come under this head. The preacher should not jump all over the platform and make a real monkey of himself. The interpreter should not scream at the top of his voice. The tongues speaker should not go thru a dozen or more gymnastics of writhing, shaking and floundering around before rising to speak. There should be a time to praise, a time to sing, a time to testify and a time to preach.

Many may be surprised to find that the Holy Spirit will so order things if He is allowed to reign supreme. God's Spirit does not anoint the interpreter to give out a message of edification and then cause a half dozen others to scream and yell and make so much noise that no one can hear or understand that message. He does not anoint the preacher to give a heaven-sent message and then anoint another or others to shake, or roll on the floor or keep up a steady stream of talking in tongues, thereby distracting the attention and breaking the spirit of the meeting. The Holy Spirit does not bring disorder, for then He would be fighting Himself, and a house divided against itself will soon fall.

However, it must not be overlooked that when the Spirit is not ruling a service and nothing but man's own thoughts and ideas are ordering the same, the Holy Spirit can and does come down upon others than those in charge and breaks thru the bondage and takes things into His own hands. But even at that, when such happens every one knows that it is God that is working.

Some one asks, "How should a service be ordered?" Let it here again be thoroughly understood that we are only speaking about the order in the general service to which the public is invited and where the gospel is preached to the unsaved. The after-meeting or private prayer meeting is a different story.

The tongues speaker should never remain seated, but should arise to his feet with as little shaking and trembling as possible, and should give his message in a clear, loud voice. The interpreter likewise should never remain seated, and without screaming or yelling should arise, and clearly and distinctly give out the message. All others should remain silent. After the messages are completed the audience should be allowed to praise or thank God, as the Spirit may move.

Tongues and interpretation should seldom be more than twice or three times. It is very seldom that the anointing is heavy enough to bring out more than three messages. Any beyond that are almost invariably in the flesh and kill the spirit of the meeting.

A message in tongues with the interpretation can come forth while a sermon is being preached under the anointing. Some question this, but nevertheless it does happen and is of God. When of the Lord it always falls in line with the message and strengthens and adds to the spirit present. Any message or manifestation that grieves the Spirit should be discouraged and if necessary forcibly quenched.

Unedifying screaming or yelling are distinctly out of order at all times, and are usually caused by headstrong individuals that more than once have received instruction and admonition. Persons who ignorantly do these things for a time or two, but who are willing to receive correction, should be dealt with gently. But others that are wise in their own conceits, and who are mulish and stubborn dispositioned, must be dealt with firmly. If they are not, it will only be a question of time before a real reign of fanaticism sets in, and once this condition is arrived at it is almost impossible to change it. If the fanatics and unruly ones will not become subject to a spirit of order, let them go where disorder reigns and there revel to the fullest enjoyment of their flesh.

This plea for order should not be used by some conceited pastor as a license for lording it over God's people or to act as a little pope that all must be subject unto. There is just as great a danger in becoming too orderly and quenching the Spirit altogether, as in becoming too loose. The first condition is often far more dangerous and deplorable than the last. A little wild fire is often better than no fire at all.

Most often the real cause of it all lies at the door of the pastor, and that in turn goes back to the spirit of the place where he received his training. No man can teach another what he does not know himself. If the pastor knows these things it is not long before the assembly profits by it. Most assemblies are just what the pastor has made them, and many never will be anything different unless the pastor changes or moves. Solid men who truly know the deep things of God are scarce and ought to be appreciated more than they are. May the Lord raise up more of them.

www.ingramcontent.com/pod-product-compliance
Lightning Source LLC
Chambersburg PA
CBHW062008220426
43662CB00010B/1267